Wild-and-Woolly

ANiMAl JokEs

An Untamed Collection of the
World's Best Animal Humor

Wild-and-Woolly
Animal Jokes

An Untamed Collection of the
World's Best Animal Humor

David McLaughlan

BARBOUR
PUBLISHING

© 2012 by Barbour Publishing, Inc.

ISBN 978-1-61626-669-1

Cartoons by Randy Glasbergen, reprinted with permission from glasbergen.com

Published by Barbour Publishing, Inc., P.O. Box 719, Uhrichsville, Ohio 44683 www.barbourbooks.com

Our mission is to publish and distribute inspirational products offering exceptional value and biblical encouragement to the masses.

 Member of the
Evangelical Christian
Publishers Association

Printed in the United States of America.

Contents

"You keep me on a chain, you make me eat on the floor, you never let me go out in public alone. We need counseling!"

Introduction

Not only did God make "all things bright and beautiful" but according to the song, He also made "all creatures great and small."

Some of those animals are bright and beautiful and some are weirdly wonderful. There are the ones with impressive wings, the ones that glow in the sea, the ones with the big teeth, awesome camouflage, impressive digestion, radar senses, horns, claws, cute whiskers, pretty pink eyes—and the ones that look like a mixture of two or three other animals!

Then, into this awesome array He put the oddest creature of all—the human being. Thankfully, He gave us the ability to laugh, and when you mix that sense of humor with the huge range of possibilities the animal kingdom offers for fun then you get. . .well. . .read on.

Be prepared to laugh, grunt, and maybe even squeak, quack, and roar!

Feathered Friends— or Pains on a Perch?

Birds soar closer to heaven than any other creature. Imagine spending most of your life soaring high above the rest of creation. . .how majestic! How awe-inspiring! But, then, birds also eat worms and make an awful mess when you least expect them to. . . .

Like mankind, birds have the ability to be both

glorious and absurd. We have beautiful birdsong and parrots talking whatever nonsense we teach them. Excuse us if we mix those two aspects—the glorious and the absurd—together in this chapter, with the balance just ever so slightly tipped in favor of the absurd, of course!

Polly Wants a Sucker!

A man went to an auction with no particular idea of what he wanted to buy, but when he saw the next lot was a beautiful parrot he decided he had to have it. After showing the bird to the crowd, the auctioneer put a cover over its cage and the bidding began.

The man had no idea how much a beautiful parrot like that was worth, but every time he made a bid someone else bid higher. More and more convinced that this must be a valuable bird he kept increasing his bid until he won.

A little concerned by the amount he had just paid, the man drew back the cover from the cage. "It is very beautiful," he said to the auctioneer. "But after paying all that money, I just hope it can talk!"

"Of course it can talk," the auctioneer said. "Who do you think was bidding against you?"

Early Risers, Late Downers

A woman liked to feed the ducks at her local pond, but after a while it occurred to her that, no matter how early she came, the ducks were always out and paddling about before she arrived.

"Yeah," said a fellow duck-feeder, "that's because they get up at the quack of dawn."

I Hope Duck Wasn't on the Menu

A duck waddled into a fancy restaurant and hopped up onto a table. Pretending she had seen it all before, the waitress brought it a menu. The duck pecked out a selection, and she brought its meal.

Once it finished, the waitress presented the duck with its check.

"Put it on my bill," it said.

Crispy Ducks

Q: What do you get when you put four ducks in a box?
A: A box of quackers.

Delicious—If You Can Catch One!

Q: Why do seagulls live by the sea?
A: Because if they lived by the bay, they would be bagels.

And in a Good Dinner Jacket, Too!

Q: What is black and white and black and white and black and white and black and white?
A: A penguin rolling down a hill.

On a Wing and a Prayer

Q: Which birds spend all their time on their knees?
A: Birds of pray.

Mock-aw

Q: Which bird is the rudest and most annoying of them all?
A: A mockingbird.

Hope the Sparrow Doesn't Mind!

Q: How does a bird with a broken wing manage to land safely?
A: It uses a sparrow-chute.

But What Is Chasing Them?

Q: Which bird is always out of breath?
A: A puffin.

You Get a Good Signal Up Those Trees

Q: How do the birds know whether they should go out in the morning or stay in their nests?
A: They watch the feather forecast.

Pecking for Coal

Q: What do you call a bird that lives underground?
A: A mynah bird.

KFO

Q: How do you know that owls are more clever than chickens?
A: Have you ever heard of a Kentucky-fried owl?

To-Wit-To-What?

The owl woke up one morning and discovered it had lost its voice. That was okay, though. The owl was a laid-back bird—and it didn't give a hoot.

Redder Robins

It was a scorching day, and two red-breasted birds decided to bask in the sun. So they lay down on the cool grass. Just then a mommy cat walked past with her two kittens.

The cats were feeling the heat as well, and the kittens mewed, "Mom! We're hungry!" and "Mom, we're too hot!"

The mommy cat looked over at the birds on the grass and said, "I know! How about some baskin' robins?"

And for My Next Trick— the Coast Guard!

A magician was part of the entertainment on a cruise ship. Knowing that the audience would be different each week, he recycled the same tricks over and over again.

There was only one problem: the captain's parrot saw all the shows. After all, a cruise ship captain's parrot doesn't get the same excitement as, say, a pirate's parrot. Having seen the tricks countless times, the parrot began to understand how the magician did them. Once it understood that, it couldn't keep it to itself. The parrot would shout things out in the middle of the show like, "Look, it's not the same hat!" or "Look, he's hiding the flowers under the table!" or "Hey, why are all the cards the ace of spades?"

The magician got angrier and angrier—but he couldn't do anything. It was the captain's parrot, after all.

One day the ship had an accident and sank in the

middle of the ocean. The magician spluttered to the surface and grabbed hold of a floating table. Seconds later the parrot fluttered down and landed beside him.

They glared at each other but, even in this situation, they refused to speak to each other. This went on all day and all night. But when the sun rose the next morning, the parrot gave up.

"Okay, okay!" it screeched. "I give up! What did you do with the boat?"

One Yellow Birdsicle, Please!

Q: What do you call a canary that forgets to fly south for the winter?
A: A brrrrrrrrrrrrrrrrrr–d!

A Dreadful Drake

Q: What do you call a duck that is always getting into trouble—and doesn't care?
A: Mallard-justed.

Hmmm?

Q: Why do hummingbirds hum?
A: Because they can never remember the words.

You're Stringing Me Along!

A man walked into a pet shop. He had a good look around, but nothing caught his attention—until he noticed the parrot. It wasn't that the parrot itself was unusual; what was unusual was that the parrot had a length of string tied to each of its legs.

Curious, the man asked the shopkeeper about the pieces of string.

"Ahh," said the shopkeeper, "just watch this!"

He tugged on the string attached to the parrot's left leg. It raised that claw from the perch and said, "Hello, handsome! Hello, handsome!"

"Cool," said the man.

"Yeah," said the shopkeeper. "And watch this!"

He tugged on the string attached to the parrot's right leg. It raised that claw from the perch and said, "My name's Pete! My name's Pete!"

The man was really impressed by this. "And what happens if you pull both strings," he asked.

The parrot looked at him and said, "I fall off the perch, you idiot!"

Parrot vs. Postman

A mail carrier had a package that required a signature. He knocked on the door and got no answer. He knocked again, and a high-pitched voice said, "Come in!"

He walked into the hallway but didn't see anyone there. "Hello!" he shouted. Again the voice said,

"Come in!" So he walked through to the kitchen—and found himself face-to-face with a snarling Rottweiler.

The mail carrier backed up against the wall and started whimpering for help. Still the voice repeated, "Come in!" He carefully edged his way along the wall, with the Rottweiler barking at every step, until he could see through a door into the next room.

There he saw a parrot in a cage. When it saw him, the parrot said, "Come in!"

Realizing he had put his life in danger because of a parrot, the mail carrier hissed, "Can't you say anything except 'Come in,' you dumb bird?"

The parrot thought for a minute. Then it shrugged and said, "Sic 'im!"

Try Flapping Your Mouth

Jake took his seat on the plane—then realized there was a parrot in the seat next to him!

Before he could get over his shock, the parrot shouted at the flight attendant, "Hey you! Get me a Coke!"

The flight attendant brought the parrot a Coke. Jake tried to get her attention, but she hurried off.

A few minutes later the flight attendant passed by again. The parrot spit some Coke into the aisle and shouted, "This is flat! Get me another one, you good-fer-nothin'! And bring me some crackers!"

Again Jake tried to ask for a drink, but the flight attendant was too flustered to notice him. She very quickly brought the parrot another Coke—but forgot the crackers.

"How did you ever get a job here?" the parrot yelled. "You're useless! Get me my crackers and get them now!"

Jake decided that rudeness was obviously the way to get results, so before the flight attendant left he yelled at her, "Yeah! And bring me a Coke, too. Right now!"

The flight attendant bustled away in tears. Then two of her male colleagues came back. They grabbed Jake and the parrot, took them to the back of the plane, opened the door, and threw them both out.

As they hurtled toward the ground, the parrot fluttered over to Jake. "Wow, man!" it said. "For someone who can't fly—you got a lotta nerve!"

Birds of a Feather Lunch Together

A parrot and a pelican went out for dinner. The pelican behaved itself—but the parrot was shocked by the size of the bill.

One Cool Parrot

Chuck had always wanted a parrot, but he made the mistake of buying one from a buddy with a challenging vocabulary. Once he got it home and encouraged it to talk, Chuck soon realized that the parrot not only had a terrible attitude, but almost every word out of

18

its beak was an expletive! Those that weren't expletives were still incredibly rude.

Chuck thought some love and kindness would help. He talked regularly to the bird, hoping it would copy some of the words he used. He even played it soothing music in the hope of calming its temper. But the parrot kept flying around, pecking holes in things, and cussing as loud as it could.

One day Chuck found it in the kitchen trying to push the window open with its beak. He tried to grab it before it could escape, and the parrot flapped him with its wings, pecked at his hands, and called him several rude names.

In desperation Chuck held the parrot's leg with one hand and reached out to open what he thought was a cupboard door with the other hand. But it was the refrigerator!

Chuck opened the door, stuffed the parrot inside, and closed the door again!

Ten minutes later, having cleaned up all the feathers, gathered himself together, and realized he had put the parrot in the fridge, Chuck opened the door.

The parrot stood, looking very contrite, on the shelf.

"I am sorry if I might have offended you in any way with my language and actions. I most humbly ask for your forgiveness, and I will make every attempt to correct my behavior." Chuck was astounded at the bird's change in attitude. He held out his arm, and the parrot jumped onto it.

"Just one more thing," the parrot said. "May I ask what the chicken did?"

Go for the Burn!

"Wow! Look at the speed of that!" said a hawk, twisting its neck to watch a fighter jet fly by.

"Pfft!" snorted the other hawk, distinctly unimpressed. "You would fly as fast as that, too, if your tail was on fire!"

Not the Country!

Q: Why did the Pilgrims eat turkey on Thanksgiving?
A: Obviously they couldn't get the moose in the oven.

A Park, of Course!

Q: What do you get if you cross a parrot with a shark?
A: An animal that talks your head off.

You Can't Vaccinate against That

Joey was really sad because his pet canary had died.

"What happened to it?" Sam asked.

"Flu," sighed Joey.

"Bird flu?" asked Sam.

"Nope," said Joey. "It got out the window and flew into a truck!"

Polly Wants a Lawyer

A lady was walking down the street to work and saw a parrot on a perch in front of a pet store.

The parrot said to her, "Hey, lady, you are really ugly." Well, the lady was furious! She stormed past the store to her work.

On the way home she saw the same parrot, and it said to her, "Hey, lady, you are really ugly." She was incredibly ticked now.

The next day the same parrot again said to her, "Hey, lady, you are really ugly." The lady was so ticked that she went into the store and warned she would sue the store and have the parrot put down. The store manager apologized profusely and promised he would make sure the parrot didn't say it again.

When the lady walked past the store that day after work the parrot called to her, "Hey, lady."

She paused and said, "Yes?"

The bird said, "You know."

The Prices Are Sky-High

Q: Where do eagles meet for coffee?
A: In a nest-café.

I Knew There Was
Something I Forgot
....

A man bought a parrot and was disappointed that it didn't talk. So he went back and asked the pet shop owner for some advice.

"Oh, it's probably just bored," the owner said. "Buy it something to distract it or excite it."

So the man bought his parrot a mirror. Still it didn't talk!

He went back to the pet shop and the shopkeeper recommended a cuttlefish shell for the parrot to peck at. The man bought it and took it home—but still the parrot didn't say a word.

The next day he bought it a ladder. The day after that, he bought it a bell to ring.

A week after he'd bought the parrot, the man went back to pet shop.

"Has it started talking yet?" the shopkeeper asked.

"Well, yes and no," the man said. "It looked in its mirror, it rang its bell, it ran up and down its ladder, it pecked at its cuttlefish, then it said a few words and fell over—dead!"

"Oh my!" said the shopkeeper. "Well, at least it spoke. Tell me, what did it say?"

The man shook his head and sighed, "It said, 'Doesn't that shop have any birdseed?'"

Ooh-La-La

A woman saw a Frenchman walking down the street with the most beautiful parrot on his shoulder. She just had to go over and say something.

"Wow! How beautiful! How elegant!" she gushed. "Where did you get him?"

"In France," said the parrot. "There's millions of them over there!"

One of These Days

"My husband races pigeons for a hobby," said one woman to the other. "It's good that it's just a hobby and he doesn't do it professionally because he never wins!"

Planting Parakeets

Billy went into the pet shop and asked for a big bag of birdseed.

"Well, how many birds do you have?" the shop-keeper asked.

"None," said Billy. "That's why I need the birdseed—to try and grow some!"

Don't Talk with Your Mouth Full

Sheila bought a parrot, but it wouldn't talk. She didn't mind too much because it was still a lovely bird, so she fed it and cared for it. About a year after she bought it, Sheila gave the parrot an apple. The parrot bit into it and then spit it out.

"Sheila!" the parrot screeched. "There's a maggot in this apple!"

"Wow!" gasped Sheila. "You can talk! Why didn't you say something before?"

"My dear lady," the parrot replied in an English accent, "I never needed to. Up until now the food has been perfectly adequate!"

Poor Man's Parrot

Jake had been looking everywhere for a parrot that could talk. But he couldn't really afford one. In the end he settled for a woodpecker that knew Morse code.

2

"Today my boss promoted me from bug to insect!"

You Can't Bug the Bugs

We tend to ignore bugs, or run squealing if we see one! But they are hugely important for the ecosystem. If mankind disappeared overnight the bugs wouldn't notice. If they were to vanish we would be in big trouble. All very admirable, but. . .well. . .some of them keep their eyes on stalks, travel on a trail of slime, bite, sting, and other weird stuff.

We might not be able to live without them, but that doesn't mean we can't have a laugh *at* them. If they wouldn't notice us disappearing they're not gonna be too "bugged" if we crack a few jokes!

Maybe They Don't
Understand the Rules

Q: Why is it better to be a grasshopper than a cricket?
A: Because grasshoppers can play cricket but crickets can't play grasshopper.

This Is a No-Fly Zone

Q: What do you call a fly with no wings?
A: A walk.

. . .And Cleopatrant?

Q: What do you call an ant with five pairs of eyes?
A: Anteneye.

Sum Body Has to Do It!

The bees' honey business was going great! They were flying honey all over the country and making a lot of money. Eventually they decided they needed someone to add up all that cash. Who did they ask to do the job?

The account-ant.

Do You Have an Appointm-ant?

The little ant was not feeling too well, so it went to a doctor. The doctor examined the ant, decided it just had a little infection—and prescribed it some ant-ibiotics.

That Ant's Older Than My Grandma!

Q: What do you call a one hundred-year-old ant?
A: An ant-ique.

A Healthy Diet Is When You Have to Work Hard to Catch Your Food

The anteater was generally considered the healthiest creature in the woods. One day a tortoise asked it the secret to its good health.

"Oh, it ain't no secret," said the anteater. "It's just that I'm so chock-full of ant-ibodies!"

Attack of the Enormous Insects

Q: What is the biggest ant in the world?
A: An eleph-ant.

Q: And what's even bigger than an eleph-ant?
A: A gi-ant.

It's Only a Small Place

Q: How many ants are needed to fill an apartment?
A: Ten ants.

How Many Legs on Those Pants?

Q: What do you call a smartly dressed ant?
A: Eleg-ant.

An Order of Aphids to Go, Please!

Q: Where do ants go to eat?
A: At a restaur-ant.

In the Department of the Ant-erior, Perhaps?

Q: What do you call an ant that works for the government?
A: Import-ant.

It'll Get a Punishm-ant

Q: What do you call an ant that skips school?
A: A tru-ant.

Bugs United

Q: What do you get if you cross some ants with some tics?
A: All sorts of antics.

Catch a Buzz

Q: What do bees do if they want to use public transportation?
A: They wait at the buzz stop.

Your Majezzzzty!

Q: What does a queen bee do when she burps?
A: She issues a royal pardon.

Just Let That Bee Be

Q: What's more dangerous than being with a fool?
A: Fooling with a bee.

Don't Make Me Sting You!

Q: What did the mommy bee say to her kids?
A: Beehive yourself.

Bees Ain't Always So Busy

Q: What buzzes, is black and yellow, and goes along the bottom of the sea?
A: A bee in a submarine.

Q: What is black and yellow and buzzes along at 30,000 feet?
A: A bee in an airplane.

Bee Charming

Q: What did the smooth-talking bee say to the pretty flower?
A: Hello, honey!

Bee-utiful!

Q: What's a bee's favorite flower?
A: A bee-gonia.

Have You Ever Seen One at the Doc's?

Q: Which bee is good for your health?
A: Vitamin bee.

!ekoJ elbirreT

Q: What goes zzub, zzub?
A: A bee flying backward.

Happy Buzz-day to You

Q: What do you call a bee born in May?
A: A maybe.

Open Your Mouth When You Buzz

Q: What kind of bee can't be understood?
A: A mumble bee.

Take Off Those Stripy Sweaters

Two bees were sitting in a sauna. One turned to the other and said, "'Swarm in here, isn't it?"

They Sit on Their Lazee-Bees

Q: What TV station do bees watch?
A: A Bee See.

Join the Buzz-sters

Q: Why did the bees go on strike?
A: Because they wanted more honey and shorter working flowers.

Who Needs Hair Gel?

Q: Why do bees have sticky hair?
A: Because of the honeycombs.

You Can Be the Bugs-Maid

Q: What did the spider say to the fly?
A: I'm getting married. Do you want to come to the webbing?

If It Bites You,
You Have a "Hot-Spot"

Q: How do you spot a modern spider?
A: It doesn't have a web, it has a website.

Catch Me If You Can!

There was a spider who really didn't like humans. How do I know? Well, it told me they drive it up the wall.

Putting Its Best Feet Forward
....

Humans have the Super Bowl, but the animal kingdom has a big sporting event as well. In a bit of an uneven match, the big animals took on the little animals in football. After the first half the little animals, not surprisingly, were being pretty well beaten, so the coach made a passionate speech to rally the little ones.

At the start of the second half, the big animals had the ball. The first play, the elephant got stopped for no gain. The second play, the rhino was stopped for no gain. On third down, the hippo was thrown for a five yard loss.

The defense huddled around the coach and he asked excitedly, "Who stopped the elephant?"

"I did," said the centipede.

"Who stopped the rhino?"

"Uh, that was me, too," said the centipede.

"And how about the hippo? Who hit him for a five yard loss?"

"Well, that was me as well," said the centipede. "So where were you during the first half?" demanded the coach.

"Well," said the centipede, "I was having my ankles taped."

Both Will Keep
You Awake at Night
....

Q: What is the difference between a flea and a wolf?
A: One prowls on the hairy and the other howls on the prairie.

Where to, Honey?
....

Q: How do bees travel when they're tired?
A: They take the buzz.

Squ-worm
....

Q: What's worse than finding a worm in your apple?
A: Finding half a worm in your apple.

What a L-ark!
....

Q: Why didn't the worms go into Noah's ark in an apple?
A: Because he said they had to go in pears.

A Bright Idea
....

Q: Why do gardeners plant bulbs?
A: So worms can see when they're burrowing underground.

That Doesn't Add Up

Q: What do bugs learn in school?
A: Moth-a-matics.

Who Wants to Be a Milli-ant-aire?

Q: What did the impatient waiter ask the greedy aardvark?
A: Is that your final ant, sir?

The Whole Basket's Moving!

Everybody knows ants are supposed to be some of the hardest working and busiest creatures in the world. So, how come they always have time to show up at picnics?

The Original Mobile Home

Q: Which animal is the strongest, an elephant or a snail?
A: The snail, of course. It carries its whole house wherever it goes. An elephant just carries its trunk.

How Rom-ant-ic!

There once was an ant that fell madly in love with an ant from another anthill. Its parents didn't approve, so it left the anthill and they both ran away to get married.

The next morning the newspaper in the anthill had a one-word banner headline—ANTELOPES.

I Found It on the Web

Q: Why did the fly fly?
A: Because the spider spied her.

Get in Step

Q: What is the longest insect in the world?
A: A centipede. Its body covers a hundred feet.

Escar Go—but Not Very Quickly

A couple was having a party at their house. An hour before the party the woman found out that she still needed escargots (snails). So she sent her husband out to get some.

He decided to walk to the market, figuring he had plenty of time. Then he bumped into an old friend he hadn't seen in a while, and they started shooting the breeze.

An hour and a half later, he looked at his watch and realized that the party had already started. He quickly ran to the market, bought the snails, and ran home. He tried to sneak in the back door without his wife seeing him, but at that moment she walked into the kitchen. He quickly dropped the snails on the path and shouted, "Come on guys! We're almost there!"

Giddy-Up, Tortoise!

Q: What did the snail say when it hitched a ride on the tortoise?
A: Wheeeee!

One Big Bouncing Bug

A Texan farmer went to Australia for a vacation. There he met an Aussie farmer and got to talking. The Aussie showed off the huge wheat field surrounding his farmhouse, and the Texan said, "They ain't nothin'! We have wheat fields ten times that size."

Then they drove an hour to the pasture area where the Aussie showed off his herd of cattle. The Texan immediately said, "They ain't nothin'! We have longhorns that are twice as large as your cows."

The Aussie farmer was getting a little tired of the Texan farmer's bragging, and the conversation died down a little. Just then a kangaroo came bouncing through the fields.

"What are those?" the Texan gasped.

"Oh," said the Aussie, seeing his chance. "Don't you have grasshoppers in Texas?"

It Hops Because
They Left the Fire On

Q: What is green, sooty, and whistles as it rubs its back legs together?
A: Chimney Cricket.

Put a Key down Its Back

Q: What is green and can jump a mile in a minute?
A: A grasshopper with hiccups.

As He Squeezes You!

Q: Where do you find giant snails?
A: At the end of a giant's fingers.

Let's Race around This Guy's
Neck and down His Shirt

Q: Two silk worms were in a race. What was the result?
A: A tie.

Flutter-highs

Two caterpillars looked up as a butterfly flew overhead.
    One of them shuddered and said, "Oh man, those thrill seekers! You'll never get me to go up in one of those things!"

High Beam

Q: What do you get if you cross a moth with a firefly?
A: A bug that can find its way around in a dark closet.

Would You Park It—
or Take It in to Show the Doc?

Jack: Imagine if tarantulas were as big as horses!
Jill: Yeah, if one bit you, you could ride it to hospital.

They Should Go Play
with the Cheetah

Q: Why can't ladybugs play hide-and-seek?
A: Because they're always spotted.

3

"Times are tough. If you want me to bring you
bird seed every morning, I have to start
charging for room service."

Bringing the
Jungle to Town

Here's an idea! Let's take wild animals and bring
them into town! Better yet, let's take them from
town to town to town!

40

Zoos and circuses have entertained and educated millions of adults and kids, but it's an idea just made for laughing at: elephants in Illinois, gorillas in Georgetown, pandas in Poughkeepsie. What are we to make of wild animals when they're out of their natural environment? And what must they make of us in ours? These jokes work both ways—and that's just the way it should be!

They Say Elephants Never Forget

Chuck was on vacation and exploring the African bush when he found an elephant wincing in pain. He noticed it was limping and spotted a giant splinter of wood sticking out of its foot. Thinking he must be crazy, Chuck carefully approached the elephant, which seemed to sense he was trying to help. Gently and carefully, he removed the splinter.

The elephant put its foot down tenderly and discovered it could walk again. It walked a few steps away then turned and looked Chuck in the eye. They held each other's gaze for a while, establishing a real bond, and then the elephant walked off into the bush.

Ten years later, Chuck went to a circus. When the elephants came in he noticed one animal in particular kept looking over at him. *I wonder. . .* he thought. *Could it possibly be the same elephant?*

He needed a closer look. So after the show he went around to the elephant compound and snuck in while no one was looking. None of the elephants paid him

41

any attention—except the one that had been looking at him earlier. It moved away from the herd, slowly walked over to Chuck, lowered its head, and looked deeply into his eyes. Then. . .

The elephant wrapped its trunk around him, lifted him up, and flung Chuck right over the circus tent.

Naw! It wasn't the same elephant.

Open Wide and Say, "Daaaaaaaaaaaaad!"

A man once applied for a job as a circus lion tamer. The ringmaster asked if he had any experience, and the man said, "Why, yes. My father was one of the most famous lion tamers in the world, and he taught me everything he knew."

"Really?" said the ringmaster. "Did he teach you how to make a lion jump through a flaming hoop?"

"Yes, he did," the man replied.

"And did he teach you how to have six lions form a pyramid?"

"Yes, he did," the man replied.

Impressed, the ringmaster went for the biggest question in the lion-taming world.

"Have you ever stuck your head in a lion's mouth?"

"Just once," the man replied.

The ringmaster asked, "Why only once?"

And the man said, "I was looking for my father."

I Don't Mime If You Don't Mime

One day an out-of-work mime is visiting the zoo and attempts to earn some money as a street performer.

However, as soon as he starts to draw a crowd, the zookeeper grabs him and drags him into his office.

The zookeeper explains to the mime that the zoo's most popular attraction, a gorilla, has died suddenly. The keeper fears that attendance at the zoo will fall off. He offers the mime a job to dress up as the gorilla until they can get another one. The mime accepts.

The next morning, before the crowd arrives, the mime puts on the gorilla suit and enters the cage. He discovers that it's a great job. He can sleep all he wants, play and make fun of people, and he draws bigger crowds than he ever did as a mime.

However, eventually the crowds tire of him, and he gets bored just swinging on tires. He begins to notice that the people are paying more attention to the lion in the cage next to his.

Not wanting to lose the attention of his audience, he climbs to the top of his cage, crawls across a partition, and dangles from the top of the lion's cage. Of course, this makes the lion furious, but the crowd loves it.

At the end of the day the zookeeper comes and gives the mime a raise for being such a good attraction as a gorilla.

Well, this goes on for some time. The mime keeps

taunting the lion, the crowds grow larger, and his salary keeps going up. Then one terrible day when he is dangling over the furious lion, he slips and falls. The mime is terrified. The lion gathers itself and prepares to pounce. The mime is so scared that he begins to run 'round and 'round the cage with the lion close behind.

Finally, the mime starts screaming and yelling, "Help! Help me!" but the lion is quick and pounces. The mime soon finds himself flat on his back looking up at the angry lion, and the lion says, "Shut up, you idiot! Do you want to get us both fired?"

A Trunk Call for Help

Jimmy had gone for an elephant ride in the zoo, but halfway through the ride the elephant handler was called away. Feeling pretty confident, Jimmy kept guiding the elephant on his own. It was great fun, until it came time to go home and he realized he didn't know the command to make the elephant kneel so he could get off.

"Hey," he shouted to anyone who would listen. "How do you get down from an elephant?"

"Well you don't, silly," a little girl replied. "Everyone knows you get down from a goose."

The Jokes Weren't That Bad!

Two lions escaped from their cage in the circus. Everyone ran as fast as they could, but the two clowns were slower than the rest (because of their giant shoes), and the lions managed to take a bite out of each of them.

One lion turned to the other and said, "Did your clown taste funny?"

I Hope the Wheels Fall off Your Car, You Clown!

A reporter was investigating a story about a lion tamer being attacked by one of his big cats. Everyone else was busy, so he got the details from the clown.

"Was the lion tamer clawed?" the reporter asked.

"He's new here," said the clown. "I don't actually know what his name is."

Waddle I Do in a Circus?

A duck walked into a diner and sat down in a booth.

The cook looked over at him and said, "Hang on! You're a duck!"

"I see your eyes are working," replied the duck.

"And you can talk!" yelled the cook.

"I see your ears are working, too," said the duck. "Now if you don't mind, can I have a coffee and a salad please?"

"Certainly, sorry about that," said the cook. "It's just that we don't get many ducks in this diner. What are you doing around here?"

"I'm working on the building site across the road," explained the duck. "I'm a drywaller."

The duck came in every day for the next two weeks.

Then one day the circus came to town. The ringmaster came into the diner, and the cook said to him, "I know this talking duck who could be just amazing in your circus!"

"Sounds good," said the ringmaster, handing over his business card. "Get him to give me a call."

So the next day when the duck came in the cook said, "Hey, Mr. Duck, I reckon I can line you up with a top job, paying really good money."

"I'm always looking for the next job," said the duck. "Where is it?"

"At the circus," said the cook.

"The circus?" said the duck, clearly confused.

"That's right," replied the cook.

"With all the animals that live in cages and performers who live in caravans?" asked the duck.

"Of course," the cook replied.

"And the tent has canvas sides and a big canvas roof with a hole in the middle?" the duck persisted.

"That's right!" said the cook.

The duck shook its head in amazement and said, "I don't get it. What would they want with a drywaller?"

He Doesn't Sit Down Much

Q: What's the name of the world's worst lion tamer?
A: Claude Bottom!

Just Send Two Mong-Ducks

The manager of a large city zoo was drafting a letter to order a pair of animals. He sat at his computer and typed, "I would like to place an order for two mongooses, to be delivered at your earliest convenience."

He stared at the screen, focusing on that odd word—*mongooses*. Then he deleted the word and added another, so that the sentence read, "I would like to place an order for two mongeese, to be delivered at your earliest convenience."

Again he stared at the screen, this time focusing on the new word, which seemed just as odd as the other one. So he deleted the word and added another, so that the sentence read, "I would like to place an order for two mongi, to be delivered at your earliest convenience."

It still didn't look right, but he couldn't think of any other words that might work. Finally, he deleted the whole sentence and started all over.

"Everyone knows," he wrote, "that no fully stocked zoo should be without a mongoose. Please send us two of them."

A Kanga-ruse

The zookeepers started work one morning and noticed the kangaroo had escaped from its enclosure. They rounded it up and erected a ten-foot fence around the enclosure.

The next morning the kangaroo was hopping around the zoo again. They put it back in its enclosure and built the fence up to twenty feet.

The next morning the kangaroo was hopping around the zoo again. And once again the zookeepers put it back in its enclosure then raised the fence to forty feet.

The kangaroo and its friend watched the workmen pack up their tools, and the friend said, "I wonder how high they're gonna go with that."

The kangaroo said, "I don't care. Just so long as they keep leaving the gate unlocked!"

Kareless Keeper

The boss of the zoo really told off one of the keepers.

Afterward one of the keeper's colleagues said, "That sounded rough. What did you do?"

The keeper said, "I left the lion's cage unlocked."

"Wow," his colleague said. "I guess that was pretty serious."

"You think so?" laughed the keeper. "Who's going to steal a lion?"

4

"The round bits taste like circles, the square bits taste
like squares, and the triangular bits taste like triangles."

Does Your Dog Bite?
Well. . .It Doesn't Bite Me!

Has mankind ever had a better friend (apart from God) than the domestic dog in all its varieties? They have lived alongside us since Stone Age days, hunting with us, protecting our homes—and getting to know all our funny little ways! No one can laugh with you and at you like an old friend can. And you get to return the favor. Which is possibly why there seems to be more jokes about dogs out there than any other animal. We know how silly and wonderful they can be. And they know the same about us!

Good Dog! Stay!

A man wanted to buy a dog, so he visited someone with one for sale. It looked like a fine dog, but he wanted to make sure.

"Is it housebroken?" he asked.

"Sure is," replied the owner.

"Can it fetch?" he asked.

"Every time," the owner said.

"And is it faithful?" the man asked.

"Absolutely!" the owner replied. "I sold him three times this week! He always comes back to me!"

A Covert Canine

A police dog was looking for more interesting work, so it went along to see the human resources guy at the FBI.

"Well," said the HR guy, "you'll have to meet some strict requirements. First, you must type at least sixty words per minute." Sitting down at the typewriter, the dog typed out eighty words per minute.

"Also," said the HR guy, "you must pass a physical and complete the obstacle course."

The dog passed the physical and completed the obstacle course in record time.

"There's one last requirement," the HR guy

continued. "Because a lot of our work means going undercover it helps to be bilingual."

The dog sat up straight, looked the HR guy straight in the eye, and said, "Meow!"

Duck, Duck!

Two guys were out hunting with their new gundog, but they weren't getting any ducks.

One guy turned to the other and said, "What do you think the problem is?"

"I dunno," his friend said. "You think maybe we ain't throwing the dog up high enough?"

Sleeping Dogs Don't Lie

A jogger stopped for a rest. Sitting down on a park bench next to an old man, he noticed a dog curled up under the bench.

"Does your dog bite?" he asked.

"Nope!" the old man said. So the jogger reached under the bench to pat the dog—and it nearly bit his finger off!

"I thought you said your dog didn't bite?" he yelled at the old man.

"He doesn't," the old man replied. "But that there ain't my dog."

It's a Dog's Life!

One day an old dog wandered into Jake's yard. The dog was wearing a collar and looked well fed, but Jake let it stay anyway and put down some food. The dog wandered over and looked at the food; then it walked over to a sunny corner, curled up, and went to sleep.

A couple of hours later the old dog woke up and wandered out of the yard.

This went on, day after day, for a week. Then as it left one day, Jake tucked a note under its collar. The note said, "Every afternoon your dog comes to my house for a couple of hours."

The next day there was a note from the owner tucked under the dog's collar. Jake opened it and read, "He lives in a house with four little children. He's probably catching up on his sleep. Can I come with him tomorrow?"

If a Dog Could Keep a Diary It Might Read Something Like This. . .

8:00 a.m.—Wow, dog food! My favorite thing!

9:30 a.m.—Wow, a car ride! My favorite thing!

9:40 a.m.—Wow, a walk in the park! My favorite thing!

10:30 a.m.—Wow, I got rubbed and petted! My favorite thing!

12:00 p.m.—Wow, bones! My favorite thing!

1:00 p.m.—Wow, I played in the yard! My favorite thing!

3:00 p.m.—Wow, I got to wag my tail for a solid hour! My favorite thing!

5:00 p.m.—Wow, dinner! My favorite thing!

7:00 p.m.—Wow, I got to play ball! My favorite thing!

8:00 p.m.—Wow, I watched TV with my humans! My favorite thing!

11:00 p.m.—Wow, I'm sleeping on the bed! My favorite thing!

Give Them a Yard and They'll Take a Howl

Joe and Joanne were desperate for a good night's sleep, but at about two o'clock in the morning the dog in a neighbor's yard started barking.

Joanne stuffed her head under the pillow and said, "I wish you would do something about those inconsiderate neighbors, Joe!"

Joe sighed. "I did talk to them. But one of them has an allergy to dogs, so they have to leave it out in the yard all night."

"Yeah, so they say," said Joanne as she jumped out of the bed. "But I don't think they care if their dog keeps their neighbors awake. I'll show them!"

Joe heard the door slam and wondered what his wife was up to. Five minutes later she was back in bed.

"That'll show them," she said.

"Show them what?" Joe asked. "I can still hear the dog barking."

"Yeah," laughed Joanne, "but I tied it up in our yard. Let's see how *they* like it!"

A Dog's Diner

A man took a dog into a diner. The manager wasn't impressed. "You can't bring that dog in here," he said.

"Ahhh," said the man. "But this is no regular dog; he can talk."

"Listen, pal," said the manager. "If that dog can talk, I'll give you and your dog a free meal."

This was just what the man had hoped for, so he put the dog on a seat and asked him, "What's on top of a house?"

The dog said, "Roof!"

"Right. And what's on the outside of a tree?"

The dog said, "Bark!"

"And who's the greatest baseball player of all time?"

The dog said, "Ruth!"

The smug man turned to the diner manager with his hand out for his free food. But the annoyed manager threw him and the dog out onto the street!

Sitting there, the dog turned to the man and said, "Do you think I should have said DiMaggio?"

Things We Can Learn from Dogs

1. Never pass up an opportunity to go for a joyride.
2. When loved ones come home, always run to greet them.
3. When it is in your best interest, practice obedience.
4. Let others know when they have invaded your territory.
5. Take plenty of naps and always stretch before rising.
6. Run, romp, and play every day.
7. Be loyal.
8. Never pretend to be something you are not.
9. If what you want lies buried, dig until you find it.
10. When someone is having a bad day, be silent, sit close by, and nuzzle them gently.
11. On hot days, drink lots of water and lie under a shady tree.
12. No matter how often you are scolded, don't buy into the pouting thing. And always be prepared to forgive at a second's notice.

How Life Works—in a Dog's Mind
· ·

When visitors arrive, quickly find out which ones are afraid of dogs. Then charge across the room at them, barking loudly, and jump up onto them. They are bound to catch you—and then fall onto the floor for more fun. This is just a maneuver to bring their faces within licking range!

When it comes to barking—that's what dogs should do. So do lots of it! Your owners will be reassured that you are a good guard dog and they will feel safe—especially in those middle-of-the-night hours! There is no more secure feeling for a human than to keep waking up in the middle of the night and hear your protective *bark, bark, bark*. . . .

Licking: Humans prefer clean tongues so always take a big drink from your water dish immediately before licking your human!

Rather than digging one big hole in the middle of the yard, which would just be dangerous, dig a lot of smaller holes all over the yard. That way there's less chance of your humans falling into one. It's simple consideration.

It's the law that the area directly in front of any door is always reserved for the family dog to sleep in.

The Art of Sniffing: Humans like to be sniffed. Everywhere. It is your duty, as the family member with the best nose, to accommodate them.

A dog puts itself to good use when guests come for dinner by always sitting under the table. This way the dog can clean up any food that falls on the floor. And it's also a good time to practice some sniffing.

Humans often talk about housebreaking, so it must be important to them. A good dog assists by breaking as much of the house as possible.

Couches: It is perfectly permissible to lie on the new couch after all your humans have gone to bed. They like you to keep it warm for them.

If you lose your footing while chasing a ball or stick, use the flower bed to absorb your fall so you don't injure yourself.

When chasing cats, make sure you never quite catch them. It spoils all the fun.

The Good Doggy Pledge

All mutts aspiring to be "good doggies" must promise. . .

- I will not play tug-of-war with Dad's underwear when he's on the toilet.
- I will not eat any more socks and then redeposit them in the backyard after processing.
- I will not chew my human's toothbrush and not tell him.
- I will not chew crayons or pens. Especially not the red ones that make people think I am dying.
- I will not roll on dead stuff.
- I will not wake Mom up by sticking my cold, wet nose up her ear.
- I will not jump through the open car window and

hightail it into the fast-food restaurant, no matter how good it smells.
- I will not throw up in the car.
- I will not bite the officer's hand when he reaches in for Mom's driver's license and car registration.
- I will not steal Mom's underwear and dance all over the backyard with it.
- I will not bark each time I hear a doorbell on TV.
- I will remember that my head does not belong in the refrigerator.
- I will try to believe my humans when they tell me the garbageman is NOT stealing our stuff.

But Only If It's a Little Dog— and Not Very Hungry!

Q: How do you catch a runaway dog?
A: Hide behind a tree and make a noise like a bone!

Its Bath Is Worse Than Its Bite

Q: What breed of dog loves to take bubble baths?
A: A shampoo-dle.

A Spring-er Spaniel, Perhaps?

Q: What kind of dog sniffs out new flowers?
A: A bud hound.

The Big Chew Toy

Q: What is the smaller dog's favorite city?
A: New Yorkie.

But It'd Talk All Day to Its Tail

Q: Why didn't the dog speak to its foot?
A: Because it'd been brought up to believe it shouldn't talk back to its paw.

The Bear-Faced Cheekiness of It!

Q: What did the cowboy say when the bear ate his faithful hound?
A: Well, doggone.

A Jaguar Chasing a Jaguar?

Q: What do you get if you cross a dog with a cheetah?
A: A dog that chases fast cars—and catches them.

You Might Need a Bigger Bun for Any Other Kind

Q: What is the only kind of dog you can eat?
A: A hot dog.

Fair's Fair—You Can Have Mine

Q: What is a dog's favorite food?
A: Anything that is on your plate.

Trash-Hounds

Q: Why is it called a "litter" of puppies?
A: Because, in no time at all, they mess up the whole house.

Does It Nip Its Own Ankles?

Q: What do you get if you cross a dog with a sheep?
A: A sheep that can round itself up.

Eee—yuckkkk!

Q: What do you get if you cross a dog with a frog?
A: A dog that can lick you from the other side of the road.

Make Sure the Squirrels
Don't Bite Your Ears
....

Frank was at his wits' end. He'd been out for a long walk in the woods with his favorite dog and, somewhere along the way, it got lost. When he got home the dog wasn't there either!

He told Buddy about his problem. Buddy walked straight to the woods. He put his ear to a tree then walked to another tree and put his ear to it. Ten trees later he had found Frank's dog.

Frank was amazed. "How did you do that?"

"It's easy, man," Buddy said. "You just put your ear to the tree—and listen for the bark!"

Check-Mutt
....

Fred was walking through the park when he saw a man playing chess with his dog. He watched the game in astonishment for a while. "I can hardly believe my eyes!" he said. "That must be the smartest dog I've ever seen."

"Nah, he's not so smart," the man replied. "I've beaten him three games out of five."

It Won a Barker!

Bobby went to the cinema the other day. He was surprised to see an old man and a dog in the front row. But he soon got distracted by the film. It was a sad-funny kind of film, you know the type. In the sad part, the dog cried its eyes out, and in the funny part, the dog laughed its head off. This happened all the way through the film. After the film had ended, Bobby decided to go and speak to the man.

"That's the most amazing thing I've ever seen," he said. "That dog really seemed to enjoy the film."

The man turned to him and said, "Yeah. Yeah, it really is amazing! He hated the book!"

What's Your Beef?

A butcher was just about to close up shop for the day when a dog strolled in. The butcher stepped out from behind the counter to shoo it away, and then he noticed it was carrying a basket.

There was a note and ten dollars in the basket.

He picked up the note and read, "Three pounds of ground beef, please."

Well, the butcher was surprised, but he saw an opportunity. So, he scooped up some of the old beef that had been around for a couple of days. The dog saw what he was doing and growled!

"Okay, okay," the butcher protested. "The good stuff it is!" And he brought some fresh meat out from the refrigerated section.

He put the beef on the scales and saw it was only about two and a half pounds.

Figuring no one would know, he went to wrap it up. But the dog growled at him until he put the rest of the beef in.

The dog reached into the basket and gave the butcher the ten dollar bill. The butcher dropped change for a five into the basket, and the dog nipped his ankle. So he dropped another five in.

Deciding he needed to know more about this animal, the butcher closed the shop and followed it. The dog crossed every road safely, entered an apartment building, pressed the elevator button with its nose, and got off at the next floor.

The butcher followed as the dog approached an apartment door and knocked on it with a paw.

When the dog's owner opened the door, the butcher just couldn't contain himself. "That's an amazingly clever dog you have there!" he said.

"Oh, you think so, do you?" the dog's owner said. "Well, let me tell you, he ain't so smart. That's the third time this week he's forgot his key!"

Why Can't Dogs Understand. . .

- Three a.m. is not the best time of day to practice barking.
- Grandma is not an intruder. You don't need to back her into a corner and guard her.
- My bed is not a big towel to dry yourself on after a walk in the rain.
- The cat has every right to be in the living room.
- Barking at guests twenty minutes after they arrive is just plain stupid.
- Every time I get up from the couch is not walk time.
- Just because I'm eating doesn't mean you can.
- If you look at me with those big soppy eyes, I'm not going to give in and feed you. NOT, NOT, NOT! Oh, okay, just this once.

If Dogs Could Write the Rules. . .

1. If I like it, it's mine.
2. If it's in my mouth, it's mine.
3. If I can take it from you, it's mine.
4. If I had it a little while ago, it's mine.
5. If I'm chewing something up, all the pieces are mine.
6. If it's mine, it must never appear to be yours.
7. If it just looks like mine, it's mine.
8. If I saw it first, it's mine.
9. If you are playing with something and you put it down, it automatically becomes mine.
10. If it's broken, it's yours.

Stop Your Yapping!

A guy saw a sign advertising a talking dog for sale.

He decided he had to find out more, so he rang the doorbell. The owner seemed really glad to see him and told him the dog was in the backyard.

The dog was just sitting there. Feeling a bit foolish, the guy said, "Can you talk?"

"Yep," the dog replied.

"So, what's your story?"

The dog looked up and said, "Well, I discovered this gift pretty young, and I wanted to help the government, so I told the CIA about my gift, and in no time they had me flying from country to country, sitting in rooms with spies and world leaders, because no one figured a dog would be eavesdropping.

"I was one of their most valuable spies eight years running. The traveling really tired me out, though, and I knew I wasn't getting any younger and wanted to settle down. So I signed up for a job at the airport to do some undercover security work, mostly wandering near suspicious characters and listening in. I uncovered some incredible dealings there and was awarded a batch of medals. Had a wife, a mess of puppies, and now I'm just retired."

The guy was amazed and asked the owner how much he wanted for the dog. The owner shrugged and said, "Ten dollars."

The guy said, "Why on earth are you selling such a fantastic animal so cheap?"

The owner replied, "He ain't so wonderful. He just made all that stuff up!"

Please Call Bark!

Q: Why are dogs like phones?
A: Because they have collar IDs.

And Around and Around and Around and. . .

Q: Why do dogs run in circles?
A: Because it's too hard to run in squares.

High, Dry Hound

Danny liked to go duck hunting with the guys. But they were all better shots than him and had all the latest equipment. Nothing Danny did ever seemed to impress them.

He decided that if he got a really good hunting dog they couldn't help but be impressed. So he searched everywhere and eventually discovered a dog that was bound to impress them. It could walk on water.

The next time they were out by the lake, a duck flew by and Danny snapped off a quick shot. Amazingly, he hit it! The dog ran out onto the lake and retrieved the duck. Only the soles of its paws got wet. But no one commented!

On the way back home Danny decided he just had to say something.

"Hey, guys," he said, trying to sound casual, "did anyone notice anything different about my new dog?"

"Sure did!" said one of the guys. "He can't swim, can he?"

Let Sleeping Dogs. . .Sleep

A salesman stopped by a country store in the middle of nowhere. As he stepped onto the porch he saw a sign on the door. It read, DANGER! BEWARE OF THE DOG!

He almost turned around and went to another store—but there weren't any for miles around, so he tiptoed up to the window and peeked in.

There was a big old hound dog sprawled across the floor. As the salesman cautiously opened the door, the hound dog opened one eye, looked at him, and went back to sleep.

"Is that it?" he asked the store owner. "Is that the dog we should beware of?"

"Sure is," said the store owner.

"Well. . .why?" the salesman asked in frustration. "He doesn't look so dangerous."

"Ohh," said the store owner, "you have no idea how many people fell over him before I put that sign up!"

He's Housebroken

A man walked into a pet store while his wife kept their son distracted outside.

"Hi," he said, "I'd like a puppy for my son."

The store owner looked out the window then said, "Well, he looks like a fine boy—but we don't do exchanges!"

What's in a Name?

Two dogs were walking along the road. One dog stopped and said, "My name is Fido. What's yours?"

The other dog thought for a minute, and then replied, "Well, according to my humans it must be Down Boy!"

Bar Cough!

Q: What do you call a big, hairy dog with strep throat?
A: A Germy shepherd.

A Dog's New Year Resolution

I will NOT run after that stick unless I see it actually leave his hand!

I Found His Weak Spot!

A timid little man walked into the roughest bar in the roughest part of town. "Excuse me, gentlemen," he said, his voice quivering with fear. "Which of you owns the Doberman tied to the No Dogs Allowed sign?"

A giant of a man wearing biker gear took a swig of his beer and turned slowly on his stool. He looked down at the quivering little man and said, "That's my dog. Why you askin'?"

"Well," squeaked the little man, very nervous, "I believe my dog just killed it. . .sir."

"You got to be kidding me!" roared the big man in disbelief. "What kind of dog do you have?"

"Well, sir," answered the little man, "it's a little Chihuahua."

"No way!" roared the biker. "How could your Chihuahua kill my Doberman?"

"Well," said the little man. "As far as I could see, he got stuck in the Doberman's throat and choked it to death."

I'll Find It in a Wee Minute

A mom was driving her kids home from day care when a fire truck went zooming past. Sitting in the front seat of the fire truck was a Dalmatian.

The children started discussing what role the dog might play in a fire situation.

"They use him to keep crowds back," said one youngster.

"No," said another, "he's just for good luck."

Then big sister joined in. "No, you sillies, they use the dogs to find the fire hydrants!"

Dog-Gone

A dog was lying on the couch watching a DVD when it felt the need to go out. It didn't want to miss any of the movie so it pressed the PAWS button.

They're Both Green and Leafy. . .No. . .Wait. . .

Q: Why is a tree like a big dog?
A: They both have a lot of bark.

Drastic Measures

A man took his dog to the vet for an examination.

The vet picked the dog up, looked, and said, "I'm sorry, but I'm going to have to put him down."

"You've hardly examined him!" the horrified man yelled. "And now you want to kill him?"

"What gave you that idea?" gasped the vet.

"You just said you would have to put him down!"

"No, no," said the vet, "I simply meant he was too heavy for me!"

One Good 'n' Gone Gundog

A city guy decided he wanted to learn how to hunt. The first thing he decided to get was a really good hunting dog, so he visited a farmer who had been advertising hunting dogs in the newspaper.

The farmer showed him several dogs, but none of them really appealed to the guy. Then, in a corner of the barn he spotted one hound the farmer hadn't shown him.

"What about that one over there?" the guy asked.

"Sorry. No chance," the farmer replied. "That one's my special dog."

"What's so special about him?" the guy asked.

So the farmer took the guy and the dog to a field to demonstrate. He lifted up one of the dog's ears and said, "Go find the birds!"

The dog ran to a nearby bush, pointed, and barked once.

"That means there's one bird in that bush," said the farmer.

"No way!" gasped the guy.

So the farmer took a stick and poked the bush until a pheasant flew out.

Seeing the guy's expression of disbelief, the farmer lifted the dog's ear again and said, "Go find the birds!"

This time the dog streaked off to another bush, pointed, and barked twice.

"That means there's two birds in there," said the farmer. He took his stick and poked at the bush. Two pheasants burst out and flew away.

The guy was mightily impressed and told the farmer he just had to have that dog. Price was no object. The farmer suggested an outrageous price, and the guy paid it willingly.

A month later, the farmer was making a trip to the city, so he decided to visit the guy who bought his special dog. When he asked the guy about the dog, the man replied, "A couple of buddies and I went hunting, and when we got to a field the oddest thing happened. I went and did what you did. I lifted one of his ears and said 'Go find the birds!'

"The dog took off like a rocket and ran into the field, barking and running around like crazy. Then he came back with a big stick in his mouth. He reached me, stood up on his hind legs, and started trying to whack me with the stick! I thought he'd gone crazy, like maybe had rabies or something. So I shot him!"

"You idiot!" yelled the farmer. "He was just telling you there were more birds out there than you could shake a stick at!"

How Many Dogs Does It Take to Change a Lightbulb?

The Border collie says—Just one. Me! And then I'll replace any wiring that's not up to code. The Rottweiler says—Make me! The Labrador says—Oh, me, me! Pleeease let me change the lightbulb! Can I?

Huh? Huh? The dachshund says—You know I can't reach that stupid lamp! The malamute says—Let the Border collie do it. You can feed me while he's busy. The Jack Russell terrier says—I'll just pop it in while I'm bouncing off the walls. The greyhound says—Is it moving? No? Who cares? The cocker spaniel says—Why change it? I can still pee on the carpet in the dark. The mastiff says—Change it yourself! I'm not afraid of the dark! The Doberman says—While it's out, I'll just take a nap on the couch. The boxer says—Who needs a light? I can still play with my squeaky toys in the dark. The pointer says—I see it, there it is, there it is, right there! The Australian shepherd says—First, I'll put all the lightbulbs in a little circle. . . . The Old English sheepdog says—Lightbulb? That thing I just ate was a lightbulb? The basset hound says—Zzzzzzzzzzzzz. . . The Westie says—Don't tell me what to do! Dogs do not change lightbulbs. People change lightbulbs. The golden retriever says—The sun is shining, the day is young, we've got our whole lives ahead of us, and you're inside worrying about a lightbulb?

The poodle says—I'll just flutter my lashes at the Border collie, and he'll do it. By the time he finishes rewiring the house, my nails will be dry.

Spot the Website

A sheepdog and a Dalmatian were sitting in an Internet café, and the Dalmatian said, "Hey, check out my website!"

The sheepdog asked for the address, and the Dalmatian replied, "Www-dot-dalmatian-dot-dot-dot-dot-dot-dot-dot-dot."

How Did You Know I Was Bluffing?

A man walked by a table in a hotel and noticed three men and a dog playing cards. He watched a while as the dog drew cards, folded, and called the occasional bluff.

"That is one very smart dog," he commented.

"Aw, he's not that smart," said one of the irked players. "Every time he gets a good hand he wags his tail."

A Felt-Tip Fido

"Dad!" yelled a little boy. "I just spotted a Dalmatian!"

"You didn't need to do that," his dad said. "He probably already had his own."

74

A Crossbreed Message?

Charlie bought a dog the other day. He called him Stay just so he could see the dog's expression when he said, "Come here, Stay!"

Bark in Time to the Beat

The town band announced it was letting animals join. The beagle wanted to play the bugle, but they didn't have one, so it settled for the trom-bone!

Smarty Pants. (Oh Yes, He Does!)

Two women were bragging about how each of their dogs was the cutest. Eventually they had to agree that the dogs were each as cute as the other. So they started bragging about how smart their dogs were.

The first woman said, "My dog is so smart. Every morning he waits for the paperboy to come around, and then he takes a newspaper and brings it to me."

The second woman yawned. "I know that," she said.

"How do you know?" the first woman asked.

The second woman smiled. "My dog told me!"

Chow Down

Q: What did the hungry Dalmatian say after he'd eaten?
A: Oh man! That really hit the spots.

If You Yawn Again, I'll Bite You!

Q: What do you call a boring dog?
A: A dull-matian.

Would Sir Like a Doggie Bag?

Q: What do you say to a dog before it eats?
A: Bone appetite.

In Search of the Perfect Bone

Q: What dog wears a white coat and does science experiments?
A: A Lab.

It's What the Best-Dressed Doggies Wear

Q: What's the difference between a well-dressed man and a tired dog?
A: The man wears a complete suit, the dog. . .just pants.

Your Dog Can Have a Room—
You Can Sleep in the Yard

A man wrote a letter to a small hotel in a town he planned to visit on vacation. He wrote, "I would very much like to bring my dog with me. He is well groomed and very well behaved. Would you be willing to permit me to keep him in my room with me at night?"

An immediate reply came from the hotel owner, who said, "I've been operating this hotel for many years. In all that time, I've never had a dog steal towels, sheets, silverware, or pictures off the walls. I've never had to evict a dog in the middle of the night for being drunk and disorderly, and I've never had a dog run out on a hotel bill. Yes, indeed, your dog is welcome at my hotel. And, if your dog will vouch for you, you're welcome to stay here, too."

You Get around the
"No Dogs Allowed" Rule

Q: What do you get if you cross a dog with a lion?
A: A terrified mailman.

First One Gets the Front!

A man bought a dachshund for his six children so they would have a pet they could all stroke at once.

Just a Tenderfoot

A dog with a bandage wrapped around one foot burst into a Wild West saloon. The room went silent, all the cowboys turned toward the dog, and it said, "I'm looking for the man who shot my paw!"

Bird Dog

Jimmy bought a dog going cheap at the pet shop. Of course, the fact that it did bird impressions made it more expensive.

It's Scary under There!

Because he lived in a high-crime area, Harry bought a dog. The shopkeeper assured him this dog would react instantly to intruders. It did. Every time it heard a noise, it instantly hid under the bed!

The One from Chihuahua?

A man said to his friend, "Our dog is just like one of the family."

"No kidding." said the friend. "Which one?"

Animal Experiment

A boy was showing off his new pet. "Hey!" he said to his friend. "Would you like to pet my new dog?"

"Well, I'm not sure," his friend said. "He looks fierce. Do you think he'll bite?"

"I don't know," said the boy. "That's what I'm trying to find out!"

Just the Sports and Comics

A man had lost his dog and was really upset about it.

"Why don't you put a notice in the newspaper?" his friend asked.

"Why would I do that?" the man asked, amazed. "My dog doesn't read newspapers!"

5

Chicken Little, Age 40.

Farmyard Funnies

The daughter of a shepherd raised a weak lamb in the farmhouse. After it got bigger and was returned to the flock, she would shout, "Rosie!" on her way to school. A single sheep would raise its head in that sea of white and say, "Mehhhh!" in reply.

Farm animals definitely have personalities of their own. That combined with the attributes that come from being a cow, pig, sheep, etc., make the farmyard a great source of jokes.

Then, of course, there are the human beings, the ones who know their way around the farm and the funnier ones who don't!

Don't Be Bossie

Harry was driving through some farming country when his car broke down. He popped the hood and looked inside, but he really didn't know much about engines. Then a deep voice from behind him said, "Mister, it sounds like you got water in your gas tank."

Harry looked around, but there was no one there, just an old brown cow munching on some grass. The cow lifted its head, opened its mouth, and repeated, "You got water in your gas tank."

Well, that was just too much for poor Harry's nerves. He turned and hightailed it up the road and across several fields until he arrived at the farmhouse.

The farmer's wife came out to see what all the commotion was. Gasping for breath, Harry told her what had happened. ". . .And then. . .a cow told me I had water in my gas tank. I must be losing my mind! What should I do? What should I do?"

"Was it an old brown cow with a white patch on its forehead?" the farmer's wife asked.

"Yeah! Yeah, that's the one!" Harry agreed.

"Hmmm." The farmer's wife thought for a moment. "Well, if I was you I'd forget all about it. That there's Bossie—and she don't know nothin' about fixin' cars!"

Real Fast Food

Sue was driving along quite happily at forty-five miles an hour when she looked out the side window and saw a three-legged chicken keeping pace with her car. More than a little surprised, she stepped on the accelerator and took her car up to fifty.

Amazingly the chicken kept up with her.

Deciding to see how fast this fantastic fowl could run, Sue increased her speed until she was cruising at seventy. The chicken kept up with her and then began to overtake her. Sue watched in amazement as the chicken sped up the street then turned left onto a dirt road.

She just had to know more about this, so she drove on up to the farmhouse and asked the farmer about the three-legged chicken.

"Well," the farmer explained, "when it comes to having chicken for dinner, usually everyone wants a leg. If there's more than two people in the family someone's bound to get left out, so we thought we'd try to address that by breeding a three-legged chicken."

"Great idea!" Sue said, watching the chicken run rapid rings around them and the farmhouse. "You must have really cornered the market. But, tell me, how does it taste?"

"Welllllll. . ." the farmer drawled. "If'n ever you catch one, maybe you could let me know."

The Yolk's on You
....

Teacher: If a rooster was perched on the top of a mountain peak with a strong wind blowing from the north, and it laid an egg, in which direction would the egg roll?

Kid: It wouldn't roll in any direction.

Teacher: Why not?

Kid: Chickens lay eggs—not roosters!

Lights, Camera, Munchin'!
....

Two goats found their way into a film studio lot. Not being fussy eaters, they nosed about in the bins and began eating a reel of film.

One goat turned to the other and said, "Hey, this is pretty good, isn't it?"

"Yeah," said the other goat. "But it's not as good as the book."

A Better Porker
....

Farmer Jones's pig had been sick for weeks. Eventually he called the vet who went into the pigsty and did his stuff.

When he went to pay the bill, Farmer Jones couldn't praise the vet enough.

"That pig was up and about within half an hour

after you left. What did you do to him?"

"Oh, nothing much," said the vet. "I just rubbed on a little oink-ment."

Moo-ve over a Bit!

Q: What do cows like to play at parties?
A: Moo-sical chairs.

Hope You Foal a Little Better

Q: What do you give a pony with a sore throat?
A: Cough stirrup.

They Like Hugh Laurie in Hen-House, MD

Q: Why do all the chickens in the barn watch TV?
A: For hen-tertainment.

Yours Sin-shear-ly

Q: What do you call sheep that live together?
A: Pen pals.

That'll Larn 'Im

Q: How do you stop a rooster from crowing on Sunday?
A: Eat it on Saturday.

Ping-Pong Ponies

Q: How do horses stay fit between races?
A: They play stable tennis.

An Udderly Ridiculous Joke

Q: What is the easiest way to count a herd of cattle?
A: Use a cow-culator.

Driving Miss Piggy

Q: What do you call a pig that's been arrested for dangerous driving?
A: A road hog.

And They Snore!

Q: Why shouldn't you share a bed with a pig?
A: Because they hog all the covers.

A Chicken Cha-Cha-Cha

Q: Which dance will a chicken just not do if it can help it?
A: The foxtrot.

Ha-Ha-Hen

Q: Who keeps all the chickens in the coop laughing?
A: Comedi-hens.

A Refridger-udder

Q: What's the best way to keep milk from going sour?
A: Leave it inside the cow.

Manners Maketh the Lamb

Q: How did the farmer know the little lamb had been
well brought up?
A: It always said, "Thank ewe," to its mom.

Don't Try This at Home

Q: What do you get if you feed gunpowder to a
chicken?
A: An eggs-plosion.

Dear Hog and Sow

Q: What does a pig use to write home?
A: A pig pen.

"Aye!" Said the Scottish Pig

Q: What do you call a pig with three eyes?
A: Piiig.

The Power of Prayer

A city dude was driving through a small town and saw a sign advertising a horse for sale. Thinking he might try something different, he found the address and knocked on the door.

The horse's owner was glad to have the sale, but he had to give a word of warning as well.

"I'm a preacher," he said, "and we are a religious family, so this horse was raised hearing words of praise. In fact, if you want him to go you have to say, 'Praise the Lord.' If you want him to stop, just say, 'Amen.'"

The city dude thought this was straightforward enough, so he took the horse and they went out for a ride.

He said, "Praise the Lord," and the horse trotted forward. Just then a truck drove past and spooked the horse, which took off at a full gallop. Seeing they were heading toward a cliff, the city dude tried frantically to stop the horse. Then he remembered the preacher's instructions. "Amen!" he yelled. And the horse stopped—right on the edge of the cliff!

The city dude drew a deep breath, wiped the sweat from his brow, and said, "Praise the Lord!"

Home (on the Range) Shopping

Did you hear about the lazy farmer who didn't want to go all the way to market to buy his livestock?

He stayed at home and bought his animals from cattle-logs.

Let's Talk Turkey

Q: What did the jewelry-loving turkey say?
A: Bauble, bauble, bauble.

Q: What did the turkey in the shoe repair shop say?
A: Cobble, cobble, cobble.

Q: What did the turkey that liked old movies say?
A: Gable, Gable, Gable.

Q: What did the turkey with a sore throat say?
A: Gargle, gargle, gargle.

Q: What did the turkey with a sore leg say?
A: Hobble, hobble, hobble.

Q: What did the football-playing turkey say?
A: Huddle, huddle, huddle.

Q: What did the dieting turkey say?
A: Nibble, nibble, nibble.

Q: What did the argumentative turkey say?
A: Squabble, squabble, squabble.

Q: What did the dizzy turkey say?
A: Wobble, wobble, wobble.

Cock-a-Doodle-Do-Don't-Do-Don't

Q: Why did the indecisive chicken cross the road?
A: To get to the other side. Ahh, no. . .to go shopping. . . well, no, not that either. . . .

Unusual? Neigh!

A traveling salesman stopped at a small town diner for breakfast. While he was waiting, he was amazed to see a horse stroll into the diner. It reared up on its hind legs—and sat down on a stool. It asked the waitress for a coffee and started to read the newspaper.

The waitress poured the horse some coffee and brought the salesman his breakfast as if all this was perfectly ordinary.

The salesman whispered to her, "Wasn't that a little unusual?"

"Sure was!" she whispered back. "He usually drinks tea!"

Who's the Donkey?
....

A successful fund manager took early retirement and decided he would like to try the country life. The country folk decided to teach the city boy a lesson, so when he bought a donkey for a thousand dollars the farmer supplied him with an old nag.

Two days later the city guy drove back to the farm. "That donkey you sold me," he said.

"Yup, what about it?" the farmer asked.

"It died!"

"Welllll," the farmer drawled, "that's a real shame."

"So, maybe you should give me my thousand dollars back."

"Probably should." The farmer smiled at him. "'Cept I spent it already."

The city guy looked at him for a moment. Then he said, "Okay," and drove off.

A month later the farmer and his friends saw the city guy again and decided to have a laugh at his expense.

"Hey!" the farmer shouted. "How's that donkey doing?"

"Well," said the city guy, ignoring their laughs. "I raffled it off."

"Who'd be foolish enough to buy a raffle ticket for a dead donkey?" the farmer asked.

"Well, several of your friends were," the city guy said. "I sold five hundred tickets at five bucks each. It covered the cost of the donkey and made me a nearly $1,500 profit."

The farmer nearly choked when he heard this.

"Didn't anybody complain?" he spluttered.

"Yeah," the city guy said. "The man who won complained."

"And what did you do?" the farmer demanded.

The city guy smiled. "I gave him his five bucks back."

Going to a Boar-ing Formal

Q: What does a pig wear to help it look smart?
A: A pigs-tie.

The Karate Pig

Q: What's a pig's favorite martial arts move?
A: A pork chop.

And That'll Be $20 for the Advice

A walker wanted to cross a farmer's field, but there was a big black bull in one of the faraway corners, so he sought the farmer's advice.

"How do you stop the bull from charging?" he asked.

"Hmm," said the farmer. "Well, usually I take away its credit card!"

I'm Quacking Up

Q: What animal goes qu-ack qu-ack?
A: A duck with hiccups.

Snort Too Difficult to Guess

Q: What do pigs do for relaxation on the weekends?
A: They go for pig-nics with their friends.

Don't Ask Silly Questions—Run!

A man climbed over a fence into a field to pick some flowers. Looking up, he noticed he was in the same field as a bull.

Seeing a farmer walking by, he shouted, "Hey, farmer! Is that bull safe?"

"Well," said the farmer, "I reckon it's a lot safer than you are right now!"

Pull the Udder One

A city man on a vacation in the country asked a farmer how long cows should be milked.

"Oh," said the farmer, giving it some thought. "Just the same way as short ones."

Have You Heard about the Dumb Tourist?

A tourist pointed into a field and said to his friend, "Look at that bunch of cows!"

A farmer was walking nearby, and he said, "Not bunch, herd."

The tourist said, "Heard what?"

The farmer replied, "Of cows."

The puzzled tourist replied, "Sure I've heard of cows."

Getting more frustrated, the farmer said, "No! I mean a cow herd."

"So what?" said the tourist. "I have no secrets from cows!"

Do You Sleep in a Barn?

Q: What farm animals do most people bring to bed?
A: Their calves.

It Had a Taste for It

Did you hear about the cow that set itself up in the yard-maintenance business?

It was a lawn moo-er.

If You Can't Get to Sleep, Count Matadors Flying through the Air

Q: What do you call a sleeping bull?
A: A bulldozer.

A Moo Hope

Q: What do you call it when cows do battle in outer space?
A: Steer Wars.

Moo-ving on down the Highway

Q: What does a cow ride when its car is broken?
A: A Cow-asaki moo-torcycle.

Psst, They're in the Barn!

Q: What happened to the lost cattle?
A: Nobody's herd.

It's Up to Moo

Q: What is the Golden Rule for cows?
A: Do unto udders as you would have udders do unto you.

There Would Be Milk Everywhere!

Q: What is the most important use for cowhide?
A: To hold the cow together.

And for My Next Trick— a Tractor into a Garage!

Q: When is a farmer like a magician?
A: When he turns his cows into pasture.

Do You Have to Feed Them Chocolate First?

Q: Where do milk shakes come from?
A: Nervous cows.

If You Don't Stop That, I'll Give You a Cow-Poke!

Q: Why did the cow tell the cowboy to leave her calf alone?
A: She thought children should be seen and not herded.

There's Nor-way You're Having Our Cows!

Q: Why doesn't Sweden export its cattle?
A: It wants to keep its Stockholm.

Bad Mews for Bessie

Q: What do you call a cow that won't give milk?
A: A Milk Dud.

Talk Turkey Instead

Q: Why should chicken farms not be built near schools?
A: To keep the students from overhearing fowl language.

Don't Say She Didn't Say

A man was driving up a steep, narrow mountain road. A woman was driving down the same road. As they passed each other, the woman leaned out the window and yelled, "Pig!"

The man leaned out his window and yelled, "Learn some manners, lady!"

She drove on and he turned the next corner—where he had to swerve suddenly to miss the hog in the middle of the road!

The Police Dogs Will Round Them Up

Q: Why did Bo Peep lose her sheep?
A: She had a crook with her.

A Team Player—All by Himself

A man accidentally drove his car into a ditch in the middle of nowhere. He hadn't seen a town in a while, and his cell phone had no signal. So he settled down for a long wait. Eventually a farmer came by, leading a tired-looking old horse.

The man asked him for help, and the farmer said Billy the horse could pull his car out. The man doubted it, but the farmer hitched Billy to the car's bumper.

Then he yelled, "Pull, Nellie, pull." Billy didn't move. Then he yelled, "Come on, pull, Ranger." Still, Billy didn't move. Then he yelled really loud, "Now pull, Fred, pull hard." Billy just stood there.

Then the farmer said, "Okay, Billy, pull!" And Billy pulled the car clean out of the ditch.

The man was very appreciative but curious. He asked the farmer why he called his horse by the wrong name three times.

The farmer said, "Oh, Billy is blind and also very lazy, and if he thought he was the only one pulling he wouldn't even try!"

Copy-Cow

There were two cows in a field, enjoying the sun and eating some grass.

The first cow said, "Moo!"

And the second cow said, "That's weird, I was just about to say that!"

Somebody Better Round Up All These Chickens

Q: Why did the chicken cross the road?
A: To get to the other side.

Q: Why did the chicken cross the playground?
A: To get to the other slide.

Q: Why did the chicken cross the fairground?
A: To get to the other ride.

And the Cockerel Won't Be Left Out Either

Q: Why did the rooster cross the road?
A: To cock-a-doodle-doo something.

Straighten Up and Fly Right, Chicken—Oh, You Can't!

Q: Why did the chicken cross the road, roll in the mud, and then go back to where it started?
A: Because it was a dirty double-crosser.

That's Just Un-clucky

Q: What happened to the chicken whose feathers were all pointing the wrong way?
A: It was tickled to death.

Ohh, They Were the Talk of the Coop!

Q: Why is it easy for chicks to talk?
A: Because talk is cheep.

Straight down the Middle

Q: Why did the chicken only half cross the road?
A: She wanted to lay it on the line.

With Their Uncles and Ants

Q: What do chicken families do on Saturday afternoon?
A: They go on peck-nics.

Hen-ny Thing You Say, Doc!

Q: Is chicken soup good for your health?
A: Not if you're the chicken.

Look Out Below!
....

Q: What do you get when a chicken lays an egg on the roof of a barn?

A: An eggroll.

6

"I don't object to being called a 'dependable workhorse'
but do you have to keep yelling 'giddyup' ?"

Giddy-Up, Dobbin!
We Got Jokes to Deliver!

If dogs have been mankind's most faithful animal
friend, then horses have certainly been their most
useful animal friend. Since the first caveman looked
at a fallen tree and wondered how he could get all
that firewood home, horses have been pulling and
ploughing and carrying for us. They let us ride on their
backs! Imagine if we had to return the favor. . . .

Having done so much for us, they probably

deserve a joke book about humans. But pages are hard to turn with hooves, so the best we can do for them is to return the favor by sharing a few laughs about horses—and ourselves!

Delighted to Beat You, My Dear Sir!

Q: How does a horse from Kentucky greet another horse?
A: With Southern horse-pitality.

D'ough!

Q: What kind of bread does a racehorse eat?
A: Thoroughbread.

Beat That!

A group of racehorses was hanging around the horse boxes after the race. With nothing much better to do, they started bragging. The first horse said, "In my last fifteen races, I've won twelve of them!"

Then the second horse said, "Well, in the last twenty-seven races, I've won twenty!"

"That's not bad," said the third horse, flicking its tail dismissively. "But in my last fifty races, I came first in forty of them!"

At this point, they noticed that a greyhound dog

had been sitting there listening.

"I don't mean to boast," said the greyhound, "but in my last ninety races, I've won eighty-eight of them!"

The horses were clearly amazed. "Wow!" said one, after a hushed silence. "A talking dog!"

Thoroughly Done Thoroughbred

An elderly lady was considering buying a racehorse, but she thought he might be getting on a bit, so she asked a veterinarian's opinion before finalizing her deal.

After the vet had completed his examination, she asked, "What do you think? Will I be able to race him?"

The veterinarian looked at the woman then looked at the horse. "Sure," he replied. "And I think you'll probably win!"

It's the Most Stable Horse on the Street

Q: What do you call a horse that lives next door?
A: A neiggghhhh-bor.

Strangely. . .It Makes Sense!

In the days when most people traveled by horse, a really tightfisted man went into a saddler's shop.

"Good morning, sir," he said to the shopkeeper. "I would like to buy a spur!"

"Certainly, sir," said the shopkeeper. "But surely

you mean a pair of spurs?"

"Do I look like the sort of man who wastes his hard-earned money?" the man demanded. "One spur, sir! If I can get one side of the horse to go quickly, the other side is bound to come along at the same speed!"

My Stable Is Your Stable

As horses say to one another, "Any friend of yours is a palomino!"

"I'll See You on the Other Side!"

A jockey was trying out a new young racehorse. After they had been around the course a couple of times, he took the horse back to the stable where the horse's owner was waiting.

"How was he?" the owner asked. "Was he well behaved?"

"Well behaved?" said the jockey. "He was so well behaved that every time we came to a jump he let me go over first!"

Cheer Up, Vet!

"Some animals are more optimistic than others," said one vet to another. "But the ones with the worst, most negative attitudes are horses."

"Why is that?" asked the other vet.

"Well," said the first vet, "all they ever say is neigh."

Cheer Up, Horse!

Did you hear about the depressed horse?
    It told a real tale of whoa!

Dude, Where's My Horse!

An office worker spent a weekend on a "dude ranch." When he came back into the office on Monday morning, his legs were bowed and he had to sit down very gently!

"Who knew something stuffed with hay could be so uncomfortable?" he sighed.

No Change

Q: What happened to the horse that swallowed a dollar bill?
A: It bucked.

Admit It, You Thought It Was a Penguin!

Q: What's black and white and turns cartwheels?
A: A piebald horse pulling a cart.

Trot, Trot, Bump

Q: What's the hardest thing about learning to ride a horse?
A: The ground.

Neigh, Surely Not!

Q: When does a horse make a noise?
A: Whinny wants to.

Just Got Hitched

Two horses arrived at a fancy hotel. At first the reception staff thought they were pulling a carriage, so they were surprised when the horses trotted into the foyer. The concierge tried to catch them and lead them back out then almost fainted when the bigger of the two horses spoke to him.

"Excuse me, my good man," the stallion said. "Would you mind getting out of the way? We'd like to book in!"

Trying to stay cool, the receptionist said, "Certainly. . .sir. Are you here on vacation?"

"No," said the stallion. "My wife and I just got married and we would like a room."

"And not just any old room," said the mare. "We'd like the bridle suite!"

They Both Fly High—
If the Horse Bucks!

Q: Why are clouds and jockeys very similar?
A: Because they hold the reins.

Ouch!

Q: Why did the boy stand behind the horse?
A: He thought he might get a kick out of it.

Its Knight Was Called Sir Fall-alot

Q: Why did the horse miss the jousting tournament?
A: It had the knight off.

Before the Others Had
Their Horseshoes On

Q: Why was the racehorse named Bad News?
A: Because bad news travels fast.

In the Land of the Blind

Q: What has four legs and sees just as well from both ends?
A: A horse with its eyes closed.

Getting a Head Start
....

A man had a racehorse that never won a race. In disgust he told the horse, "You win today or you'll be pulling a milk wagon tomorrow morning."

The starting gate opened and the race began. All of the horses ran like they were jet-propelled. All except one!

The owner jumped onto the track and found his horse sleeping in the stall.

"Why are you sleeping?" he yelled.

The horse yawned and opened one eye. "I have to be up at three in the morning," he said.

7

"Sixty percent of your DNA is exactly the same as an Oreo cookie."

Over the Hills
and Far Away

There's no place on the globe that mankind cannot
go with enough expensive equipment. But when
he gets there he usually finds nature has beaten him to
it. Animals live on the highest mountains and in the
coldest polar regions with nothing to protect them but
their own fur coats—oh, and some serious claws and
teeth.

So what must they think when they see a hiker

or explorer coming along in several layers of brightly colored, protective clothing with all the latest expedition equipment? How about, "My! Dinner sure looks fancy tonight!"

I Can't Bear to Hear You Argue Like This
....

The mountain creatures were arguing about which of them was the most awesome.

The hawk claimed that because of its ability to soar high above everyone else and its ability to swoop down on its prey it ought to be him. The others grudgingly admitted the hawk was pretty impressive.

But the mountain lion insisted it was the most powerful creature in the mountains. It could climb, stalk, and pounce. Its jaws and claws were well nigh inescapable. The others thought the mountain lion had a good case.

Then the little skunk argued that it ought to be considered. After all, even though it didn't have big claws or fierce talons every animal in the mountains was scared of getting sprayed by the skunk.

But while they had all been so busy talking about themselves, none of them had noticed the bear listening from behind a tree. Deciding to settle the argument once and for all, the bear leapt out and ate them. It swallowed them hawk, lion, and stinker!

It's There in Black and White

Q: Why was the little bear so spoiled?
A: Because its mother panda-d to its every whim.

B the Best That You Can B!

Q: What do you call bears with no ears?
A: B.

Who's Skinning Who?

Two men went bear hunting. They spent the night in a cabin in the woods. One guy got up and set out bright and early while his companion snoozed. He soon found a huge bear. He took aim and shot at it—but he missed! The enraged bear charged toward him, so he dropped his rifle and started running for the cabin as fast as he could.

He ran pretty fast, but the bear was just a little faster and gained on him with every step. Just as he reached the open cabin door, he tripped and fell flat. Too close behind to stop, the bear tripped over him and went rolling onto the cabin floor.

The man jumped up, closed the cabin door, and yelled to his friend, "You skin this one while I go and get another one!"

Look Out for That—Never Mind!

Q: What do you call a deer with no eyes?
A: No-eye deer.

Making a Bear Is No Pic-a-nic

Q: Why did God make only one Yogi Bear?
A: He wanted to make more, but when He tried again He made a Boo-Boo.

It's Just Not Fur!

A daddy bear and a baby bear were walking across the Arctic Circle when the baby polar bear said, "Dad, am I part panda bear?"

"No," replied his dad.

"Well then, am I part grizzly bear?" Again his dad said no.

A short time later the baby bear asked, "Dad, am I part koala bear?"

The father said, "Look, son, I'm a polar bear, your mom's a polar bear. Why do you think you are part anything else?"

"Because," the baby bear said, "I'm completely freezing!"

Would You Like
Them Super-Sized?

A polar bear walked into a fast-food restaurant. Standing at the counter, it said, "I'll have a cheese-burger. . . . . .and fries."

"Why the big pause?" asked the guy behind the counter.

The polar bear looked down at its hands and said, "What do you mean? I've always had them."

It's a Brrr!

Q: Why did the grizzly bear get a cold?
A: Because it went out in its bear feet.

Uncle Bill's Cool, Too

Q: What is a penguin's favorite relative?
A: Its Aunt Arctic.

Pushy Penguins

Q: What's black and white, black and white, black and white. . . ?
A: A penguin rolling down a hill.

Q: What's black and white and rolling around laughing?
A: The penguin that pushed it.

A N-ice Idea

A man wanted to buy a pet but was shocked at the cost, especially the cost of pet food. Eventually the exasperated pet shop owner suggested he get a polar bear as a pet.

"Why?" asked the man.

"Because," said the pet shop owner, "everyone knows they live on ice!"

The Pack Wants a Snack

Q: What holiday do wolves celebrate in the fall?
A: Howl-oween.

Bear with It, Owl!

Q: Everyone thinks the owl is wise, but most of the woodland animals go to the grizzly bear for answers. Why?
A: Because it has the bear facts.

Oops, She Made a Boo-Boo

A man walked into a diner with a little blue bow tie–wearing bear. When the waitress asked if they wanted anything to drink, the man said, "I'll have an orange juice, and he'll have a Mattabooboo."

Confused but curious, the waitress looked at the

little bear and said, "What's a Mattabooboo?"

The little bear looked up in surprise and said, "Nuttin', Yogi!"

One Brave Seal!

A polar bear decided it wanted one of those cozy, dome-shaped homes the Inuit have. But it couldn't figure out how they managed to make sure all those blocks of snow didn't fall into a heap.

Another bear came along and said, "I'll tell you how they do it if you'll let me share the shelter."

"Hmmm. All right then," said the first bear. "How do they do it?"

"It's obvious," said the second bear. "They stick them together with i-gloo!"

Bare Bear

Q: Which animal are you most like when you get out of the bath?
A: A little bear.

Get Bear-ligion!

A hunter was in the middle of the forest, many miles from anywhere, when he suddenly walked into a surprised grizzly bear. When they recovered their wits, the hunter dropped his rifle, turned, and ran while the grizzly chased after him, getting faster and faster.

The hunter burst out of the woods only to find himself at the edge of a cliff. The grizzly pushed two trees aside and advanced, growling and baring its teeth.

"God," the hunter prayed, "help me, please!"

Just then the grizzly stopped. The hunter realized that even the birds in the air and the wind in the trees had stopped. God's face appeared in the clouds and said, "Hi!"

The stunned hunter managed to gulp out a feeble "Hi" in response.

"So, let Me see if I've got this right," God said. "You've never believed in Me. In fact, you have mocked people who do believe in Me. But now, in your time of greatest need, you expect Me to think you've got religion. Is that about right?"

Now, the hunter was foolish, but he wasn't hypocritical. He realized he couldn't deny God all his life and then ask God to do something for him. He said as much to the Almighty.

"Maybe there's another way," the hunter said. "I can't in good conscience ask You to do something for me. But You could do something for the bear!"

"Hmmm?" said God.

"Yeah! You could give *it* religion—that'd be doing it a big favor," said the hunter. *And that might keep it from eating me*, he thought to himself.

"Done!" said God. He disappeared in a flash, and the bear began to look stunned.

The hunter was sure he would be safe now. The

bear walked toward him and raised its arms as if to say, "Hallelujah!" Then it brought them together in prayer and said, "For the food I'm about to receive, may the Lord make me truly thankful!"

Make Your Own Then You Won't Have to Worry!

Once upon a time there were three bears that lived in a cottage in the woods. Coming back from a walk, Papa Bear noticed something unusual.

"Who's been sleeping in my bed and left the covers all messed up?" he roared.

The baby bear ran into his own room. "Who's been sleeping in my bed and left the covers all messed up?" he squeaked.

Mother Bear walked in and said, "Will you two calm down? I just haven't had a chance to make them yet!"

Was It a Combination Lock?

Q: How did the moose keep its antlers from being stolen?
A: It locked horns with another moose.

This Will Definitely Hurt

Q: What do you call a vaccination given to a boy deer?
A: Buck shot.

Chew on This

Q: What do you call a grizzly bear with no teeth?
A: A gummy bear.

8

"After the hunt, could you stop off and get me
some zebra nuggets and a gazelle shake?"

Tarzan's Garden—
It's a Jungle Out There!

If you want a glimpse at the amazing diversity of
creation then step into a jungle—but be careful
where you step! A mind-boggling variety of plants and
animals coexist there in an amazingly chaotic harmony.
Despite everything seeming to be poisonous, hungry,
or tasty, it just works. That's because everything there
has its place in the Grand Scheme.

Then along comes Twenty-First-Century Man.

He's not made for the jungle—but he's not gonna let that stop him. So, let the jokes begin!

You're the King—
or Am I Lion to You?

One morning the lion woke up determined to show the rest of the animals just who was the boss. Strolling through the jungle, he grabbed a monkey by the tail and pulled it from the tree. "Who's the king of the jungle?" he roared.

"Y–y–you are, oh mighty lion!" the monkey said.

Walking past the mud wallow, the lion spotted a warthog. "Who is the king of the jungle?" he roared. Sinking down into the mud, the warthog whimpered, "You are, oh mighty lion!"

Jumping in between a giraffe's legs, the lion roared up, "Who is the king of the jungle?" With its knees knocking, the giraffe squealed, "You are, oh mighty lion!"

Wondering who else was going to be unlucky enough to get in his way, the lion found some elephant tracks. Running up behind it, he jumped onto the startled elephant's back and roared, "Who is the king of the jungle?"

The elephant whipped its trunk back, wrapped it around the lion, and knocked him against several nearby trees before letting him go. Only just managing to stand up and stagger away, the lion shouted back, "Okay, okay! No need to be grumpy just because you don't know the answer!"

Pray You Don't Meet Daniel. . .or Samson

There was an old lion that people guessed must have been cared for by a missionary when it was a young cub.

Why did they think that?

Because before the old lion and the rest of the pride went hunting it always gathered them together and said, "Let us prey!"

That Joke Was a Bit Off

One day a lion pounced on a group of celebrities on safari. The actor, the singer, and the professional speaker all got away, but the lion gobbled up the comedian.

It felt funny for days after that.

Abraca-tiger!

Q: When is a tiger not a tiger?
A: When it turns into its cage.

And They Drink on Thirst-day

Q: On which day do lions eat people?
A: Chews-day.

A Family Cat

Q: What do you call the lion that ate your mother's sister?

A: An aunt-eater.

Design by God

Q: If a four-legged animal is a quadruped and a two-legged animal is a biped, what is a tiger?

A: A stri-ped.

Shere Khan Knew What It Felt Like

Q: What's the difference between a wet day and a hurt tiger?

A: One pours with rain, the other roars with pain.

Home, Stripy Home

Q: Who can go into a tiger's cage and come out ten minutes later without a scratch?

A: The tiger.

Why Little Boys Wish They Were Leopards

Q: Why wouldn't the leopard take a bath?
A: It didn't want to get spotlessly clean.

Over There!

The leopard kept trying to sneak out of the zoo, but it was no use. It was always spotted.

Cute 'n' Crafty

A Valley Girl decided to go on an African safari with some friends, figuring it would be good for her tan. She took her bag dog, Cuddles, along because she never went anywhere without him.

Cuddles quite enjoyed the freedom and the wide open spaces, but before long he realized he was lost. Worse than that, there was a leopard creeping up on him!

But just because he was cute didn't mean he was dumb. Cuddles noticed a pile of bones nearby. He strolled over and started chewing on one. Then, loud enough for the sneaky leopard to hear, he said, "That sure was one delicious leopard. But I'm still hungry. I wonder if there are any more like that around here."

Whoa! thought the leopard. *That mutt must be tougher than it looks. I'm outta here!*

As the leopard ran back into the jungle, a sly monkey, that had seen everything, decided to stir up some trouble—and get the leopard to owe it a favor. So, swinging from tree to tree, the monkey took off after the big cat and explained everything. The leopard was furious and immediately turned back.

Cuddles saw the leopard returning with the monkey on its back and quickly figured out what was going on. He knew he couldn't outrun the leopard, so he had to do some quick thinking.

As the leopard crawled closer, Cuddles rolled onto his back and sighed, "That monkey is so slow. I sent it to get me another leopard ages ago!"

Strangely, no one ever saw that monkey again!

Not Bananas, Then?

Q: What is a monkey's favorite snack?
A: Chocolate chimp cookies.

Rock-a-Bye, Monkey

Q: Where do mommy gorillas keep their babies?
A: In ape-ri-cots.

Japes in the Jungle

Q: Which day of the year do mommy and daddy gorillas dread?
A: Ape-ril Fools Day.

Mind You Don't Slip

Q: How do young chimps get down the stairs?
A: They slide down the banana-ster.

The Key to Good Nutrition

"Humans think it's easy to open a banana," the mommy chimp said to her children. "And it is for them with their little, thin fingers. But we have a better way!"

"What's that, Mom?" one of the children asked.

"Well, little one," the proud mom said, "we open our bananas with a mon-key!"

What Happens If You Don't Have Tall Enough Traffic Lights

Q: What do you get when two giraffes collide?
A: A gi-raffic jam.

Jungle Rules

Q: Why don't the jungle animals play too many competitive games?

A: Because the place is full of cheetahs.

A Biiiig Difference

Q: What is the difference between an elephant and a flea?

A: An elephant can have fleas but a flea can't have elephants.

Don't Sit Up Too Quickly

Q: How do you know when there is an elephant under your bed?

A: It's a bit of a giveaway when you're lying in bed and your nose touches the ceiling.

Can You Get a Trunk in the Overhead Compartments?

Q: What do you call an elephant that flies?

A: A jumbo jet.

Boing! Thump! Boing! Thump!

Q: What do you get if you cross an elephant with a kangaroo?
A: Big holes all over Australia.

Can I Have an Elephant Smoothie, Please?

Q: Why are elephants wrinkled?
A: Have you ever tried to iron one?

Seems a Shame to Waste Ears Like That

Q: Why do elephants never forget?
A: Because nobody ever tells them anything.

Always Obey the Rules— or the Gorilla Will Get You

Bob had a gorilla as a pet. It was well trained but had never been left on its own. So when he had to go to the hospital for a while, Bob asked his neighbor, Rocky, to look after it for him.

Rocky said, "Sure," and Bob told him all he needed to know about caring for the gorilla; how to feed it, exercise it, clean out the cage, and so on. "But never, ever, ever touch it!" Bob warned.

So when Bob went to the hospital, Rocky swung

into action. A few days later, after he gave the gorilla a banana, it occurred to him that it might be nice to pat the arm of such a well-behaved gorilla. That fur looked nice and smooth!

He couldn't get over not being able to touch the gorilla. There didn't seem to be any reason not to, and after a week of doing what Bob told him Rocky gave in to temptation. As he passed the gorilla another banana, he let the back of his hand brush against the gorilla's fur.

Suddenly the gorilla went ape and started to jump up and down. Then it got a crazy look in its eyes and started walking slowly and deliberately toward Rocky.

Rocky ran from the house, slamming the door behind him. The gorilla ran right through the door.

Rocky jumped into his car and floored the accelerator. Breathing a sigh of relief, he glanced into the rearview mirror. The gorilla was in Bob's car and gaining on him!

Rocky drove desperately until his car ran out of gas. He jumped out, ran into an alley, jumped a wall, then climbed into a Dumpster where he buried himself in garbage and tried to silence his thumping heart.

The lid of the Dumpster creaked open, and a great big hand brushed the garbage off him. Rocky looked up fearing he'd breathed his last and wishing he had taken Bob's advice.

Two big, bloodshot eyes looked down at him. Then a massive finger tapped him on the forehead.

"Tag!" said the gorilla. "You're it!"

There He Is!

Q: Why can't a leopard play hide-and-seek?
A: Because it's always spotted.

Q: Why does the tiger have stripes?
A: So it can play hide-and-seek without being spotted.

Charms the Savage Beast

A famous violinist figured he was such a good player that his music could even tame the wildest of beasts.

To prove his theory he set out deep, deep into the jungle. Finding a clearing, he unpacked his violin and began to play. First a few birds fluttered down to see what the beautiful noise was. Then the zebras and antelope came along. A few snakes, a cheetah, and some hippos came along. Then a rhino nosed its way into the clearing. Even the lions and tigers joined in. And they all stood there, engrossed in the music. Not one thought of running away, not one thought of giving chase, and not one thought of eating any of the others!

Then an old crocodile swam up the river and crawled onto the bank behind the violinist. Closer and closer it came. Then with a mighty snap it gobbled the violinist up!

With the music gone, all the animals started shouting at the crocodile, asking why it had done that.

The old crocodile lifted one front foot up to its ear and said, "Eh?"

Ouch! Oh No. . .

Two snakes were slithering through the swamp when one asked the other, "Are we the venomous kind of snake or the other kind?"

The other one replied, "Oh boy, are we venomous! We are the most venomous kind! Why'd you ask?"

To which the first replied, "Ohhh, I was really hoping we were the other kind. I just bit my tongue!"

Watch Out for the Landing!

Q: What's big, gray, and flies straight up?
A: An ele-copter.

But It Ate Your Grapes!

Q: What's gray, brings flowers and chocolates, and cheers you up when you're ill?
A: A get well-ephant.

A Long Way Lost

Q: What's the difference between an African elephant and an Indian elephant?
A: About 3,000 miles.

Does That Shell Have a Parachute?

A contented crocodile was lazing around in the watering hole one day when it saw an elephant come down for a drink. Coming to the edge of the water, the elephant stopped. There, sleeping on a rock, was an old turtle. The elephant bent down and examined it closely. Then it reared back onto its hind legs and kicked the turtle so hard it flew at least a mile through the air.

"What did you do that for?" the crocodile asked.

"Well," said the elephant, "about fifty years ago that turtle bit my foot. Today I finally found him again and paid him back."

"Fifty years!" gasped the crocodile. "But that's a long, long time. How could you be sure it was the same turtle?"

"Ohh," the elephant replied, "I have turtle recall."

Sssssssso Funny

Q: How can you tell if a snake likes your joke?
A: It laughs hisssssss-terically.

They Really Snap It Up

Q: What does an alligator get on welfare?
A: Gatorade.

A Jungle Hot Spot

A hungry lion was on the prowl for a good meal. Coming to a clearing, it saw two men. One was sitting under a tree reading a book; the other was sending messages on his phone.

The lion quickly pounced on the first man and devoured him. Then it strolled away leaving the other man untouched. Why?

Because even the king of the jungle knows that readers digest and writers cramp!

Go Faster Stripes

A man was on safari with a really obnoxious guide. Wandering away from camp with no weapons one day, they spotted a tiger. Worse than that, the tiger spotted them!

The man reached into his pack and pulled out a pair of top-notch running shoes.

"You've got to be kidding me," the panicking guide spluttered. "Do you really think those shoes are going to make you run faster than that tiger?"

"I don't have to run faster than the tiger," the man replied. "I just have to run faster than you."

Really Marking Your Man

It was a boring afternoon in the jungle, so the Elephants decided to challenge the Ants to a game of soccer. The game was going well, with the Elephants beating the Ants ten goals to nil, when the Ants gained possession.

The Ants' star player was dribbling the ball toward the Elephants' goal when the Elephants' left back came lumbering toward him. The elephant trod on the little ant, squishing him.

The referee stopped the game. "What do you think you're doing?" he yelled at the elephant. "It's not exactly sportsman-like to kill your opponent!"

"Well, I didn't mean to kill him," the elephant replied. "I was just trying to trip him up!"

Don't Put Me on Hold, Anna Conda!

A man phoned 555-JUNGLE. When the operator came on the line, he said, "Get me the king of the beasts!"

The operator replied, "I'm sorry, sir, the lion is busy."

Should've Turned Left at Norway

Q: What do you call a polar bear in the jungle?
A: Lost.

Otherwise You Will Be a Light Snack

A group of tourists was about to head out on safari with their guide, but one of them was determined to show the others how much he knew about the jungle. After delaying the departure for about half an hour by telling them all the jungle lore he had learned on the Internet, he turned to the guide and said, "And isn't it true that carrying a flashlight will save you from being eaten by lions?"

"I suppose so," said the guide. "But it does rather depend on just how quickly you can carry it!"

Tarzan—He Never Went to School, You Know!

Q: What did Tarzan say when he saw a herd of elephants in the distance?
A: "Look, a herd of elephants in the distance!"

Q: What did Tarzan say when he saw a herd of elephants with sunglasses?
A: Nothing. He didn't recognize them.

Q: What did Tarzan say when he saw a group of raccoons?
A: "Ha! You fooled me once with those sunglasses, but not this time!"

It Was the Coolest Party Around!

Q: How do you get an elephant into the fridge?
A: Open door. Insert elephant. Close door.

Q: How do you get a giraffe into the fridge?
A: Open door. Remove elephant. Insert giraffe. Close door.

Q: The king of the jungle decided to have a party. He invited all the animals in the jungle, and they all came except one. Which one?
A: The giraffe, because it was still in the fridge!

Tell the Tooth

Q: The cheetah might cheat, but what animal never tells the truth?
A: The lion.

It's a Tale of Whoa!

Q: Where did the zebra go when the tiger bit off its tail?
A: The re-tail store.

Flying on a Jumbo, of Course

Q: Why did it take the elephant so long to get on the airplane?

A: Because it had to check its trunk.

Birds Beware!

Q: What is three stories tall and moves at 20 mph through the jungle?

A: A giraffe on rollerblades.

To Go!

Two tigers were relaxing under a tree when an antelope accidentally walked past them. Seeing them there, it took off like a rocket!

"Hey!" said the first tiger. "What was that?"

Watching the antelope disappear over the horizon, the second tiger sighed and said, "Fast food!"

Use a Tissue!

Q: Why do gorillas have such big nostrils?

A: Have you seen the size of their fingers?

Just Popping Out for a Quick Bite

Q: What is a lion's favorite part of the school day?
A: LUNGE!

And Stretch!

Q: Why do giraffes have such long necks?
A: Because their feet smell really awful.

Its Banana Was Split

Q: What did the monkey say when it fell out of a tree?
A: Ooo-ooo, aah-aah. . .ow-ow!

The Sssesssesssion of the Sssouthern Sssstatesss, Perhapsss?

Q: What is a snake's favorite lesson?
A: Hisss-tory.

Monkeys in a Bath— Ohhh, the Mess!

There were two monkeys in a bath. One jumped up and down and said, "Oo-oo, ah-ah!"

The other one said, "Well, put cold water in then!"

Katie 1—Tiger Nil

Tommy was trying to scare little Katie. "Imagine you were in the jungle and a tiger was creeping through the undergrowth and was about to eat you all up! What are you gonna do?"

Katie rolled her eyes at how easy this was. "Duh," she said. "I'm gonna stop imagining!"

That "Hiss" Was a Leak!

A snake went to see the optician because it was having problems with its eyes and wasn't as good at biting people these days.

The optician tested its eyes and fixed the snake up with a pair of contact lenses. "These should help," he told the snake. "Try them out and come back in a few weeks."

The snake came back in two weeks. Its success rate in biting people had gone right up since it had the lenses fitted. But now it needed a doctor to deal with its depression.

"How long have you been depressed?" the optician asked.

"Ohh," sighed the snake. "Since I left here two weeks ago and discovered I'd been in love with a garden hose for the past six months!"

How Did the Elephant Get in Your Home in the First Place?

"My homework is really difficult tonight," Caleb said to his dad. "I have to write an essay on an elephant."

"Well," said his dad, scratching his head. "For a start you're going to need a ladder!"

That Trunk Flies Cargo

"When an elephant squirts water from its trunk," said Billy, "is it really powerful, do you think, Nate?"

Nate thought about it for a moment then said, "Well, I once heard a jumbo jet can keep five hundred people in the air for hours!"

Tut, Tut, Teacher!

The teacher asked Kayla, "Where would you find an elephant?"

Kayla sighed and shook her head. "It's not so important where you find them. What I want to know is how you could lose something so big in the first place!"

Maybe It Should Wear Sneakers

Q: What do you call an elephant creeping through the jungle in the middle of the night?
A: Russell.

How Do You Hide One of Those under Your Pillow?

Q: What is gray, has a wand, huge wings, and gives money to elephants?
A: The tusk fairy.

A Smart Car Would Have Gotten Out of the Way

A rich man drove his fancy car into the jungle and then got out to take some photos with his expensive camera. While he was looking in the other direction, a tired elephant stumbled into the same clearing. Seeing the car there and mistaking it for a big black rock, the elephant sat down on it.

What do you think happened next?

Well, everybody knows Mercedes Bends!

Tell Him He Has Big Ears

Q: What is the easy way to get a wild elephant?
A: Get a tame one and really annoy it.

Imagine How Elephants Must Snore!

An elephant was having trouble sleeping at night so it decided it had to do something about it. The next day the elephant's friends commented on how well rested it looked.

"You must have had a really good sleep," one said.

The elephant smiled and nodded, and the others wanted to know how it had managed it.

"Easy!" said the elephant. "I went to the vet and he gave me some trunk-quilizers!"

Just Stand between the Four Gray "Trees"

Q: What's big and gray and protects you from the rain?
A: An umbrella-phant.

Keeps Elephants Away—Far Away!

A woman was sprinkling a powder all around her immaculately kept garden.

"Excuse me, ma'am," a neighbor's daughter asked. "What's that you're doing there?"

"Well, honey," the woman explained, "I heard that elephants are particularly fond of these kinds of flowers. So, I'm sprinkling anti-elephant powder."

"Ma'am," said the girl, hesitantly, "I don't think

there are any elephants in America."

"Exactly!" said the woman. "This powder is real good stuff!"

Just a Little Monkey Business

A guy was walking down a street one afternoon when he passed an old man sitting on the side of the road with a large sack. It seemed to be moving around a lot!

He said to the old man, "What you got in the sack?"

The old man responded, "I got some monkeys in that there sack."

He then asked, "If I guess how many monkeys you got in the sack, can I keep one?"

The old man replied, "Son, if you guess how many monkeys I got in this sack, I'll give you both of 'em!"

Drink Up and Grow Big

Kenny: Did you hear about the baby that was fed on elephant's milk? It gained twenty pounds in three days!

Jenny: Wow! Whose baby was it?

Kenny: The elephant's.

It Answers Its Phone and the One Six Operators Away

Q: What do you call a monkey that works in a call center?
A: A who-rang-utan.

Too Much Sugar in Its Diet

Q: What's white and swings through the trees?
A: A mer-angutan.

Just Get Out of the Way!

Q: What's big and gray and has sixteen wheels?
A: An elephant on roller skates.

Slow, Slow, Ouch, Ouch, Slow

Q: Why are four-legged animals bad dancers?
A: Because they actually have two left feet.

They Were Also the Bal-last

Q: What animals were last to leave the ark?
A: The elephants because they had to pack their trunks.

Al's Not Well

Q: What do you call a sick alligator?
A: An ill-igator.

And As for Brushing His Teeth Afterward. . .

Q: Why was the little elephant six hours late for dinner?
A: It had to wash behind its ears before coming to the table.

King Louis Style

Q: What kind of music do monkeys like?
A: Swing.

It's Supposed to Be a Non-Contact Sport

Q: What's an elephant's favorite racquet sport?
A: Squash.

9

**"Tomatoes, corn syrup, vinegar, water, salt.
See, there are no cats in catsup!"**

Cuteness—with Claws!

Cats! What can you say about them that they wouldn't correct if they could talk? They are often as cute as can be, lovely to come home to—and they also keep down the mice. But you do get the feeling that they are only ever visiting, that they are doing you a favor by looking after you.

So until we find out what their master plan really is, let us love them, stroke them, and enjoy an occasional joke at their expense. But *never* let them know you are laughing at them. . .their revenge will be swift and overwhelming!

United Pussycat Service

Q: Why did the mother cat put stamps on her kittens?
A: Because she wanted to mail a litter.

S-cat Nav

A man had no idea a cat could be such an annoyance when his wife brought the cute little kitty home. But after months of it scratching his stuff and sinking its claws into his ankles, he'd had enough. It was time for the cat to go!

So he put it in the car, drove a few blocks away, found a park, and left the cat there. When he got back home he was amazed to find the cat sitting on his chair purring happily.

The next day, he put the cat back in the car and drove out of town. He threw the cat into a field and sped back home. But when he walked back into the house the cat was already on his chair purring.

More determined than ever, the next day he put the cat in the car and drove. . .and drove. . .and drove!

Deep in the mountains, he shoved the cat out into

the snow and turned the car around.

Two hours later he phoned home, and his wife answered.

"Hey, honey," he said, "is the cat there?"

Confused by the question, his wife said. "Sure she is. She's sitting on your chair."

"Well," said the man in a strangled voice, "can you put her on the line? I'm lost and I need directions home!"

Mee-ack!
·················

Q: What do you call a cat that swallows a duck?
A: A duck-filled fatty-puss.

Cat Laws
·················

Isaac Newton discovered many of the Laws of Thermodynamics. But Isaac Caton discovered the Laws of Catodynamics, which are—

1. The Law of Inertia, which states that a cat at rest will tend to remain at rest, unless acted upon by some outside force—such as the opening of a can of cat food, or a nearby scurrying mouse.
2. The Law of Motion, which states that a cat will move in a straight line—if there's a dog on its tail. In which case, that straight line will go straight over any walls, cars, and humans that may get in its way.

3. The Law of Magnetism, which states that dark clothes will attract cat hairs in direct proportion to how much the wearer dislikes cats.

Smooth, Not Crunchy

Q: What is a cat's favorite pudding?
A: Chocolate mousse.

A Message from the Humans

Dear Cats,

The dishes with the paw print are yours and contain your food. The other dishes are mine and contain my food. Please note that placing a muddy paw print in the middle of my plate of food does not make it your food or your dish. And I won't smile and say, "Aw, how cute!"

The stairway is not a racetrack or an amusement park ride. Beating me to the bottom is not the object. Tripping me is not some sweet way of helping me to win!

I cannot buy anything bigger than a king-sized bed. I am very sorry about this. Just because there are lots of you and only one of me does not mean I will keep on sleeping on the couch. Nor do I like the idea of sleeping in your empty baskets. Cats can actually curl up in a ball when they sleep. It is not necessary to sleep perpendicular to each other stretched out to the fullest extent possible. Stretching your tails out and letting your front paws loll over the comforter does not entitle you to extra space!

For the last time, there is not a secret exit from the bathroom. If by some miracle I beat you there and manage to get the door shut, it is not necessary to claw, whine, meow, or try to turn the knob or get your paw under the edge of the door to pull it open. I must exit through the same door I entered. There is nothing going on in there that you need to know about or that I need your help with!

And finally—and I cannot stress this enough—the proper order is kiss me, and then go and sniff the other dog or cat. Not the other way around!

Thank you! Meow!

Followed by the Weather Fur-cast

Q: What is a cat's favorite TV show?
A: The evening mews.

Look Out, It's a Pet-quake!

Q: Black cats are said to be unlucky, but what's the unluckiest kind of cat to have?
A: A catastrophe.

Get the Latest Pet on Twelve Monthly Installments

Q: What do you get if you cross a cat with a tree?
A: A cat-a-log.

Band-Aids and Balls of Yarn

Tiddles the cat had heard about an earthquake in South America. The Red Cross was calling for donations to buy equipment, so Tiddles went along and told them he knew CPR and artificial respiration.

"Why are you telling me this?" the confused aid worker asked.

"Because!" said Tiddles. "Your advertisement said you needed more first-aid kits!"

Cat-sup with That?

Q: What do you get if you cross a cat with a bottle of vinegar?
A: A sourpuss.

They Milk It for All Its Worth

Q: How do you know that cats aren't easily upset?
A: They never cry over spilled milk.

Snap!

Q: How do you spell "mousetrap" in just three letters?
A: C-A-T.

Woolly Kitties

Q: What happened to the cat that swallowed a ball of
  yarn?
A: It had mittens.

A Cat versus Dog Worldview

A dog thinks: *Hey, these people I live with feed me, love
me, pet me, take good care of me, and provide me with a
nice warm, dry house. . . They're sooo wonderful!*

A cat thinks: *Hey, these people I live with feed me, love
me, pet me, take good care of me, and provide me with a
nice warm, dry house. . . I must be sooo wonderful!*

They Wanted to
See the Stat-chews

Q: Where did the kittens go on their school field trip?
A: To the mew-seum.

...And Go
....

Q: What do you call it when a cat stops for a second?
A: A paws.

2 for 1
....

A neighbor looked over the garden fence and saw little Billy filling in a hole in the lawn.

"Hey there, Billy!" he called over. "What you doing there?"

"Burying my goldfish," Billy sobbed.

The neighbor kept quiet for a moment out of respect, but his curiosity got the better of him.

"That's an awful big hole for a little goldfish," he observed.

"Yeah," said Billy, patting the last of the dirt into place. "That's because he's inside your big greedy cat!"

Talk Doggish
....

A mother mouse and a baby mouse were walking along when, suddenly, a cat jumped out onto the path in front of them.

The mother mouse could have escaped, but the cat would certainly have caught the baby, so she stood her ground and started barking like a dog. The cat got the fright of its life and ran away.

"What did I tell you?" the mother mouse said to

her baby. "Now do you see why it's important to learn a foreign language?"

How to Use Up Those Nine Lives

Q: What swings from a trapeze and doesn't need a safety net because it always lands on its feet?
A: An acro-cat.

So Says the Cat

Q: Which animal makes the best pet?
A: Cats, because they are purrrrrrr-fect.

Me-owrange?

Q: What's a cat's favorite color?
A: Purr-ple.

Cat Rules (or Cats Rule?)

- Aquariums are just interactive television for cats.
- Anything on the ground is a cat toy. Anything not there yet, will be.
- Dogs do what you tell them to do. Cats take a message and get back to you.
- Buy a dog a toy and it will play with it forever. Buy a cat a toy and it will play with the wrapper for ten minutes before ignoring the toy and the wrapper forever.

- No matter what they've done wrong, cats always try to make it look like the dog did it.
- Cats bite the hand that won't feed them fast enough.
- Cats are smarter than dogs. You couldn't get any number of cats to pull you on a sled through the snow.
- Cats instinctively know the exact moment their owners will wake up. Then they wake them ten minutes earlier.
- Cats know what their owners feel. They don't care, but they know.
- Dogs have owners. Cats have staff.
- Dogs believe they are human. Cats believe they are better than that!
- If your partner or children are allergic to cats—get a new family!
- In a cat's thinking, all things belong to cats.
- People who hate cats will come back as mice in their next life.
- Some people say that cats are sneaky, evil, and cruel. And they have many other fine qualities!
- There are many intelligent species in the universe. All owned by cats.

How to Wash the Cat
....

One day a pet-owning couple found the following note on their porch—

THE CAT NEEDS A BATH

1. Thoroughly clean the toilet.
2. Add the required amount of shampoo to the toilet water.
3. Find the cat and soothe it while you carry it toward the bathroom.
4. In one smooth movement, put the cat in the toilet and close both lids. (You may need to stand on the lid so that the cat cannot escape.) The cat will self-agitate and make ample suds. Never mind the noises that come from your toilet, the cat is actually enjoying this. CAUTION: Do not get any part of your body too close to the edge of the toilet seat, as the cat's claws will be reaching out for anything they can find.
5. Flush the toilet three or four times. This provides a power wash and rinse cycle, which I have found to be quite effective.
6. Have someone open the door to the outside and ensure that there are no people between the toilet and the outside door.
7. Stand behind the toilet as far as you can and quickly lift both lids.
8. The now-clean cat will rocket out of the toilet and run outside where it will dry itself.

It was signed—
THE DOG

Soggy Moggies

A cat in England and a cat in France heard that they had the same name only, in their different languages, the English cat was called One Two Three while the French cat was called Un Deux Trois.

A rivalry rose up between them about who was the best, so they arranged to race each other across the English Channel. They both got off to good starts and eventually the One Two Three cat made it to the other side. But the Un Deux Trois cat sank!

(Un, Deux, Trois, Quatre, Cinq. . . .)

We Won't Paws Till It's Done

A guy walked into a laundry and, to his amazement, he discovered it was run by cats. "Excuse me," he said to the cat in charge, "can you get milk stains out of this jacket?"

"Sure," replied the cat. "We'll have that stain licked in a minute!"

With All the Mews That's Fit to Print

Q: What do cats read in the morning?
A: Mews-papers.

Whassat? Asleep?
I Was Never Asleep!

Q: What do you call a cat two seconds after the alarm clock goes off?
A: Catsup.

They Get Lots of Fish

Q: What do you call a cat with eight legs that likes to swim?
A: An octo-puss.

Obviously Not
Jean-Claude van Cat

Q: What do you call the cat that loses a hissing, scratching cat fight?
A: Claude.

Not a Good Idea!

Q: What do you get if you cross a cat with a parrot?
A: A carrot.

Mildly A-mewww-sing

Q: What do cats put in their drinks on hot days?
A: Mice cubes.

From the Meow Tse-tung Period

A famous art collector was walking through the city when he noticed a mangy cat lapping milk from a saucer in the doorway of a store. That's when he did a double take. The saucer, even though it didn't look like much, was a very valuable Chinese antique. So he walked casually into the store and offered to buy the cat for ten dollars.

The store owner replied, "I'm sorry but that there is an expensive cat."

The collector said, "Please, I need a hungry cat around the house to catch mice. I'll pay you fifty dollars for that cat."

And the owner said, "Sold," and handed the cat over.

Almost as an afterthought the collector said, "Hey, for that fifty bucks I wonder if you could throw in that old saucer. The cat's used to it, and it'll save me from having to get a dish."

And the owner said, "Sorry, buddy, but that's my lucky saucer. So far this week I've sold sixty-eight cats!"

You Need the Farm Shop, Mister!

"Have you got any kittens going cheap?" asked a customer in a pet shop.

"No, sir," replied the owner. "All our kittens go meow."

Where Would You Get a Litter Box Big Enough?

A driver accidentally ran over a cat one day. Distraught, he checked the tag for a phone number. Then he called the owner and explained what had happened. After apologizing about a hundred times, he said, "Please let me replace the cat for you!"

The owner said, "Well, I appreciate the offer, but are you really any good at catching mice?"

That's Right!

"My cat's so smart," said Eddie to his friend, "he can even do math! Why, just yesterday I asked him, 'What's six plus six minus twelve?' And he said nothing!"

10

**"Good morning and welcome to
my productivity seminar..."**

The Menagerie
of Mayhem

Nobody's going to argue if the jungle animals
want a chapter of their own. They have tusks
and claws and other fierce stuff. And the doggies and

pussycats have been part of our lives for so long they kinda deserve their own chapters. But what about the aardvark and the camel and the skunk? What about all the little fluffy creatures who live in cages in our bedrooms? Who's going to argue for them?

We are! Which is why we have gathered them all—and others like them—together in this menagerie of mayhem. Enjoy!

My Fellow Hamsterians

Q: What do you call a hamster with a top hat?
A: Abraham-ster Lincoln.

Hammy's European Vacation

Tired of endlessly going around on its exercise wheel, a hamster decided to book a vacation. Then after reading through some travel brochures its owners had lined its cage with, the hamster found the perfect place.

Where was it? Hamsterdam.

Hare Today, Gone Tomorrow

Jimmy was depressed, so his buddy tried to get him to tell what the problem was.

"It's something I've got," said Jimmy. "Something

everyone must have noticed by now, but I just can't bring myself to say the words."

"Describe it then," his buddy said.

"Okay," sighed Jimmy. "It's like five hundred big rabbits hopping backward into the distance."

His buddy was puzzled for a moment then he realized: "Oh! You have a receding hare line!"

A Good Place for a Hoppy Tale

A rabbit hopped into a library and up onto the librarian's desk. In a little squeaking voice she explained that she had lots of children and they wanted her to read them bedtime stories. Could the librarian recommend any?

"Well, what kind of stories do they like," the librarian asked.

"Oh," the mommy bunny squeaked, "ones with hoppy endings."

Taste-ful

Q: What did the bunny give his girlfriend when he asked her to marry him?
A: A thirteen-carrot ring.

Beware of the Pet Owner

A note to all pet haters visiting this house. Remember:
1. They live here. You don't.
2. If you don't want their hair on your clothes, stay off the furniture. (That's why they call it fur-niture.)
3. I like my pets a lot better than I like most people.
4. To you, it's an animal. To me, he/she is an adopted son/daughter who is short, hairy, walks on all fours, and doesn't speak clearly.

Why Pets Are Better Than Kids

1. They eat less.
2. They don't talk back to you. Or if they do, you never understand it.
3. They are so much easier to train.
4. They come when they are called. (Unless they have found something really disgusting and smelly.)
5. They never pester you for the car keys.
6. They aren't interested in the latest expensive fashions.
7. They can go to pet training classes, which are way less expensive than college.
8. They would prefer a stick or a ball of yarn over a laptop or a game station every time.
9. They always love you—no matter how un-cool you might be.
10. If they get too big for the house—you can sell them!

Bunny McFerrin

Q: What was the Jamaican bunny's motto?
A: Don't worry, mon, be hoppy.

Ur-bunn

Q: What is a rabbit's favorite dance style?
A: Hip-hop.

Will They Go to Burrow-bados?

Q: Where do rabbits go after their wedding?
A: On their bunny-moon.

State of Inde-pet-dence

Q: Which state has the most pets?
A: Pet-sylvania.

It Says So in the Book

A panda strolled into a restaurant, sat down, and ordered a sandwich. It ate the sandwich then pulled out a gun and shot a hole in the ceiling.

The panda started to leave, and the manager shouted after it, "Hey! You just shot up my restaurant and you didn't pay for your sandwich! Who do you think you are?"

The panda turned around and said "Hey man, I'm a panda! Look it up!"

The manager opened his dictionary and read: "Panda. A tree-dwelling marsupial of Asian origin, characterized by distinct black and white coloring. Eats shoots and leaves."

You Have Sore Fingers, Too? Snap!

The boys' mother looked crossly at her sons as she put Band-Aids on their scratched fingers. "Well," she said, "I hope you two have finally learned never to go near snapping turtles at the pond."

One of the boys replied, "Yes, ma'am. It really tortoise a lesson."

Water in the Desert

Q: What do you call a crying camel?
A: A humpback wail.

A Hundred-Acre Smell

Q: What do you get if you cross a skunk with a teddy bear?
A: Winnie the Phew.

Heat Up the River, Please!

Q: What's the best animal to be on a cold day?
A: A little otter.

You'd Have to Be Batty to Do That

A vampire bat flew back into the cave with blood all over its face. Thinking it must have found some docile animals and had a good feed, the other bats gathered around excitedly.

"Where did all that blood come from?" they asked.

"Well," it said, "you know when we fly out of the cave?"

"Yeah! Yeah!" the other bats said, excitedly.

"And you know how we always turn to the left?"

"Yeah! Yeah!" the other bats said.

"Well, I turned right."

"Yeah? Yeah?"

"Yeah," the bat said, "and flew straight into a great big tree!"

No Roaring during the Examination, Please!

"I think animal testing is a terrible idea," said little Janie. "The poor things would all get really nervous and write down the wrong answers."

You'd Be Nuts to Be Anything Else

A baby rabbit was left on its own in the woods. Without parents to look after it, things were looking a bit desperate. Fortunately, a family of squirrels decided to adopt it.

Its bunny teeth were good for eating nuts, but as the rabbit grew it began to notice more and more differences between itself and its squirrel brothers and sisters. For instance, while they liked to run around in tree branches, the rabbit preferred the ground.

Eventually fearing it was somehow not good enough to be a real squirrel, the little rabbit talked to its squirrel parents. They could see that this had become a big problem for their adopted child. They talked about it among themselves and eventually decided the best thing to do was to tell the rabbit to be true to its own nature.

So they said, "Don't scurry! Be hoppy!"

Hold on Tight, Baby!

Q: Why does a koala carry its baby on its back?
A: Have you ever tried pushing a stroller up a tree?

Nighttime—You're Out!

Q: What animal is good at baseball?
A: A bat.

Someone Open a Window—Quick!

Q: How many skunks does it take to stink up a room?
A: A phew.

Emily Hams It Up

Emily wanted a hamster, but her mom didn't think it was a great idea. So Emily pestered and pestered and pestered and, eventually, Mom gave in. But she made Emily promise she would take good care of her new pet.

And Emily did—at first! For the first few weeks, looking after the hamster was a novelty, but eventually it began to wear off. Gradually her mom started doing the feeding, the cleaning of the cage, and so on.

One day when Mom already had too much to do she shouted at Emily, reminding her of her promise and pointing out how badly she'd kept it.

"How many times do you think this poor hamster would have died by now if it hadn't been for me looking after it?" Mom asked.

"Ohh, I don't know," Emily replied. "Once?"

Eggs-actly the Right Thing to Do
....

A man was driving along the highway, enjoying the sunshine and the music on his radio. Suddenly something big, white, fluffy, and carrying a basket ran out from the bushes and onto the road in front of him.

There was a thump, and the front of his car was splattered with chocolate eggs.

The driver pulled over to the side of the road in shock. But through his shock came the horrifying realization that he must surely have killed the Easter Bunny.

Scared to look out and wondering what it would be like to have all the kids in the world hating him, he just sat there trying to get himself together.

A moment later another car pulled up behind him. The woman driving it got out of her car and came to see if he was okay. Still shaking, he told her all about driving into the Easter Bunny.

"Oh my!" she said. Then she patted his arm and told him it would be okay, she knew exactly what to do. She went back to her car and returned with a spray can. Then she emptied it all over the part of the road where he guessed the Easter Bunny lay.

Two minutes later the Easter Bunny popped up. It straightened its big ears, picked up its basket, and hopped away. When it got fifty yards down the road it turned and waved. Fifty yards farther, it waved again. Another fifty yards, and another wave.

"Wow!" the man shouted. "That was amazing!

What did you do?"

"Ohh, nothing much," the woman said. "I just happened to have some of this."

She held out the spray can, and he read on the label, "Hair spray. Restores life to dead hairs. Adds a permanent wave."

Cute—and About to Pop

Q: What's small and cuddly—and purple?
A: A koala bear holding its breath.

It's Ard Vaark Raising Critters

A man wanted a new aardvark, so he looked through the classified ads. He called one number, and a woman answered.

"How much are your aardvarks?" he asked.

"They're ten dollars each," she replied.

"Did you raise them yourself?" the man asked.

"Sure did," the woman said. "Yesterday they were only eight dollars each!"

Just Give It Your Ants and Run

Q: What do you call a thick-skinned aardvark?
A: A hard-vark.

Another Three Inches and He Would Be a M-eater

Q: What do you call a three-foot-long aardvark?
A: A y-aardvark.

A Pept-Abysmal Joke

Q: What does an aardvark get when it overeats?
A: Ant-digestion.

It's Three O'Clunk!

Hickory, dickory, dock, the mouse ran up the clock. The clock struck one—but the rest got away.

Mind Your Head, Cat!

Q: What are gray, squeaky, and hang by their tails from the roofs of caves?
A: Stalag-mice.

And the Cat Gets a Tune-Up

Q: Why do mice need oiling?
A: Because they squeak, of course.

Bee for Bunny

Q: A cheeky bee was chasing a rabbit. Finally the bee turned around and flew away. Why?
A: The rabbit already had two *b*'s.

Look Out Burrow!

Q: Why did the rabbit clutch a basket full of eggs as it jumped off the bridge?
A: It was the Easter Bungee.

Hop on In

Q: How far can a rabbit run into the woods?
A: Only halfway. After that it's running out of the woods again.

The Bunny Bakes Buns

Q: What do you call a rabbit that bakes a lot of bread?
A: A yeast-er bunny.

Don't Mock the Platypus

Q: What's the difference between a duck-billed platypus and a bowl full of lettuce?
A: One is a funny beast and the other is a bunny feast.

A Buffalo Bump

Q: What happens when two oxen bump into each other?
A: It is reported as an ox-ident.

Talk about Chasing Your Tail!

You are in an unusual situation.

On your left is an ostrich. On your right is a gazelle being chased by a lion. In front of you are two deer. Behind you are three stampeding horses.

What's the safest thing to do?

Get off the merry-go-round.

Bargains at the Pet Shop

A hummingbird that knows the words.
A bloodhound with hay fever.
A chameleon that's stuck on green.
A depressed hyena.
An absentminded elephant.

All the Gifts Were Cheesy

Q: How do mice celebrate when they move into a new home?

A: With a mouse-warming party.

It's a Bit Tight in This Burrow for the Both of Us

Q: What do you call spending the afternoon with a cranky rabbit?

A: A bad hare day.

So, That's All the Time Then?

Q: When do squirrels chase people?

A: When they think they're nuts.

11

"According to the encyclopedia, we should have grown legs
and evolved into land creatures millions of years ago.
Why didn't we get a memo about this?!"

Better Where
It's Wetter

Wasn't it a certain Disney lobster that said things
are better where they are wetter? It certainly
is an amazing and mostly undiscovered world down
there in the ocean. Perhaps things aren't necessarily
better, but they most certainly are odder. Where else
would creatures with eight arms mingle with creatures
with no brains (and no, I'm not talking about humans
there)?

So let's dive deep into the ocean with the blue

whale and crawl onto land with the adventurous frogs, and we will see if the jokes at least are better where it's wetter!

Going for a Walk-topus

A boy and a girl octopus were out on their first date. With the evening sun shimmering through the shallow water, they strolled along the seafloor arm in arm in arm in arm in arm. . . .

Buddy, Can You Spare Some Slime?

The octopus was collecting money for a good (undersea) cause, and all of the fishy creatures were giving generously.

"Except for that pair of oysters over by the reef!" the octopus complained.

"Ahh, don't take it personally," the dolphin reassured him. "They never give to any good causes."

"Why not?" the octopus asked.

"Ohhh," the dolphin sighed, "they're just two shellfish!"

I Wouldn't Go to His Place

Did you hear about the fish dealer who never gave anyone a little extra and never let anyone off with a dime?

Twenty years in the business had made him sell-fish.

Eye Have No Idea

"Hey!" said the old fisherman to the young angler. "What do you call a fish with no eyes?"

"I don't know," said the young angler. "What do you call a fish with no eyes?"

"A fsh."

Krypto-goldies

Q: Where do Superman's goldfish live?
A: In the Super Bowl.

Fish Food, Now! Or Else!

There were two goldfish in a tank, and one asked the other, "Do you know how to drive this thing?"

Those Must Be Some Damp Dollars

Q: Where do fish get their money from?
A: The riverbank.

Weigh to Go, Fishy!

Q: Why is it easy to weigh fish?
A: Because they always have scales.

A Ticket to Somewhere Deep, Please!

Q: How do you find out how heavy a whale is?
A: You take it to a whale-way station.

Yikes! I Buried It on the Beach!

When you move as slowly as a turtle, it means meeting up with friends can take an impossibly long time. But they do manage to keep in touch. They use their shell phones.

Salute, Salute, Salute, Salute...

Q: What would be a good career for an octopus?
A: The arm-y.

It Shelled Out Some Cash

Q: Where did the turtle get a new shell?
A: From the hard-wear store.

Shoal-ly Not!

Q: Why are fish so smart?
A: Because they spend most of their time in schools.

Sounds Like a Fishy Tale to Me

After a good day out fishing on the lake, a fisherman was heading toward the parking lot carrying two brown trout in a bucket. Just as he was about to drive away, a fisheries officer walked over and asked to see his permit.

He didn't have one, but he did some quick thinking.

"I wasn't fishing," he said to the fisheries officer, "and I didn't catch these trout. In fact, they aren't even wild trout—they are my pets. Every day I come down to the lake and dump these fish into the water and take them for a walk to the end of the pier and back. When I'm ready to go I whistle, and they jump back into the bucket, and we go home."

The fisheries officer was not convinced and started talking about how much the man could be fined for fishing without a permit.

"Hey, sir," the man protested. "If you don't believe me, I can show you!"

He looked convincing, and the fisheries officer was just a bit curious, so after a moment's hesitation, he said, "Okay. Show me!"

The man took his bucket to the lakeside and poured the fish into the water. Then he and the fisheries officer took a leisurely stroll to the end of the pier and back. Arriving back, the fisheries officer said, "Okay, now whistle to your fish and let me see them jump out of the water and into the bucket."

The man kept walking toward the parking lot. "Fish?" he said. "What fish?"

I Haven't Heard This Joke Before

A goldfish was gliding through its castle and around the treasure chest when it spotted its human coming over to the fish tank with some fish food.

Oh no! Fish flakes again, he thought. *Just because I have a tiny memory span they think they can keep on feeding me the same stuff over and. . . Oh boy! Fish flakes! I can't remember the last time I had them!*

Pop in for a Bite Any Time

Two fishermen were walking back from the lake at the end of the day. One said to the other, "Did you get many bites today?"

"Sure did," the other fisherman replied. "I got fifty-three."

"Fifty-three!" the first fisherman gasped. "That's an amazing number!"

"Yeah," sighed the other fisherman. "One fish and fifty-two mosquitoes!"

A Bridge over Troubled Fishes

Two fish were swimming in a river when it began to rain.

"Quick," said one fish to the other, "let's swim under that bridge so we don't get wet!"

Forever in the River

A man was strolling along a riverbank when he stopped to talk to an angler.

"Is this river any good for fish?" he asked.

The angler replied, "It must be. I've been here all day and I can't get any of them to leave it."

Stop Spouting Off

Q: What do you do with a blue whale?
A: Try to cheer it up.

Humans! There's Something Fishy about Them

Q: How do you know dolphins are intelligent?
A: Within a few weeks of captivity they can train a man to stand on the edge of their pool and throw them fish three times a day.

Not Thirsty

A mom asked her son if he had put fresh water in his fish's bowl recently.

"Didn't think I should," the boy said. "It hasn't finished the last lot yet."

Hitch-hopping?

A man was cruising down the road when he saw something small and green by the edge of the asphalt. Getting a little closer, he saw it was a frog. Closer still and he saw the frog had its thumb in the air.

So he pulled over, opened the door, and said, "Hop in!"

Unless They Are Geckos

Q: What kind of tiles can't you stick on walls?
A: Rep-tiles.

I'm Toad-ally Sorry

Q: What happened to the frog when it parked illegally?
A: It got toad away.

Perhaps a Wildlife Book— or a Joke Book!

A chicken came into the library, stopped in front of the librarian, and said, "Buk, buk, BUK!" The librarian tried to shoo it away, but the chicken kept coming back and saying, "Buk, buk, BUK!"

Eventually, with no other clue as to what to do, she decided the chicken must want a book. So she gave it a romance.

The next day the chicken came back, stopped in front of the librarian, and said, "Buk, buk, BUK!" Rather than go through the whole thing again, she gave the chicken a thriller. It took the book and left.

When the chicken came in the third day and said, "Buk, buk, BUK!" she gave it a sci-fi book and followed it as it left.

She followed it out of town to a pond where the

chicken seemed to throw the book into the water. But a frog caught it before it got wet, looked through it, and then threw it back.

"Reddit!" the frog croaked.

No Wonder It Sounds So Hoarse in the Morning

Q: They say cats have nine lives, but what animal has more lives than a cat?
A: A frog, it croaks every night.

One Bug Meal a Day

Q: Why are frogs usually happier than humans?
A: Because they eat whatever bugs them.

Froggy's Femur

Q: How did the frog feel after it broke its leg?
A: Pretty un-hoppy.

Who Knew Frogs Could Do Math?

Q: Why do frogs like years that are divisible by four?
A: Because they are leap years.

It Needs an A-pond-ectomy

Q: Why was the frog in the hospital?
A: To have a hop-eration.

Hop In or Take Away?

Q: What did the frog order from the drive-thru?
A: Fries and a croak.

Don't Bug Momma

Two young frogs were down by the pond catching bugs. They had been there most of the day when their momma called them to bed.

"Wow!" said one frog to the other. "Time's sure fun when you're having flies!"

One Slightly Damp Muppet

Q: What do you get if you cross a frog with some mist?
A: Kermit the Fog.

It'll Jump to Get You

Q: What do you get if you cross a steer with a tadpole?
A: A bullfrog.

12

"Actually, I'm a litigator."

Real Animal Laws— Supposedly!

Be fiercer than the other guy—or be faster than him!" That would do for a basic law of the jungle. But that's obviously far too simple for human beings. We have to complicate things.

So we bring animals into our world and then

make laws for them. Now surely that's only fair if we give the animals the chance to go to law school and defend themselves, right? Imagine! Donkeys and wolves practicing law and owls sitting in judgment. Hmmm.

Until then, laws for animals are just silly, and that's the way we like them!

• Cats in International Falls, Minnesota, are not allowed to chase dogs up telephone poles.
• In Belvedere, California, no dog is allowed in a public place without its master on a leash.
• In Arvada, Colorado, if a stray pet is not claimed within twenty-four hours, the owner will be destroyed.
• In Barber, North Carolina, fights between cats and dogs are against the law.
• In Sterling, Colorado, it is unlawful to allow a pet cat to run loose without a taillight.
• Cats living in Cresskill, New Jersey, must wear three bells to warn birds.
• In Fountain Inn, South Carolina, the law once required horses to wear pants.
• In Charleston, South Carolina, carriage horses were required to wear diapers.
• In Winona, Mississippi, it is illegal to drive a car on Main Street because it frightens horses.
• In Wilbur, Washington, it is against the law for a person to ride an ugly horse!
• In California you are not allowed to keep farm

animals in your apartment.

- In Cumberland, Maryland, you cannot keep chickens in your hotel room.
- In Minnesota it's illegal to tease skunks.
- In Atlanta, Georgia, it's against the law to tie a giraffe to a telephone pole or a streetlight.
- In Nevada it is illegal to ride a camel on a highway.
- In North Carolina it is illegal to take a deer swimming in water above its knees.
- In North Carolina it is against the law to use elephants to plough cotton fields.
- In New York City it is illegal to shoot rabbits from a streetcar when it is moving.
- In Kansas people are not allowed to shoot rabbits while in a motorboat.
- In Statesville, North Carolina, it is against the law to race rabbits in the streets.
- In Tuscumbia, Alabama, no more than eight rabbits can reside on the same block.
- In Detroit, Michigan, it is illegal to tie a crocodile to a fire hydrant.
- In Brooklyn, New York, donkeys are not allowed to sleep in a bathtub.
- In Baltimore, Maryland, it is necessary to document any work done by a jackass.
- In Ohio it is against the law to set a fire under your mule.
- In Marshalltown, Iowa, a horse will be breaking the law if it eats a fire hydrant.
- In Oklahoma people can be fined or jailed for

making ugly faces at a dog.

- In Chicago, Illinois, it is illegal to take a French poodle to the opera.
- In Wallace, Idaho, it is unlawful for a human to sleep in a dog kennel.
- In Clawson, Michigan, a law specifically makes it legal for a farmer to sleep with his pigs, cows, horses, goats, and chickens. But the animals may not be in the house after sunup or during the day.
- In Florida livestock must not be transported on school buses.
- In Alabama no mules can be traded after supper when the sun has already gone below the horizon.
- In Idaho you can't buy or sell chickens after sundown without the sheriff's permission.
- In Tennessee and Washington State it is illegal to lasso a catfish.
- In Seattle, Washington, goldfish can ride the city buses in bowls only if they keep still.
- In Louisville, Kentucky, you cannot shoot fish with a bow and arrow.
- In Oklahoma it is against the law to get a fish drunk.
- In the state of Washington it's illegal to catch a fish by throwing a rock at it.
- In Norfolk, Virginia, it is illegal for hens to lay eggs before 8 a.m. and after 4 p.m.
- In Essex Falls, New Jersey, ducks are legally required not to quack after 10 p.m.
-
- In Quitman, Georgia, it is actually against the law

for a chicken to cross the road.

- In Massachusetts, fowl, particularly roosters, are prohibited from going into bakeries.
- In Kansas it is illegal for chicken thieves to work during daylight hours.
- In Pennsylvania no one is allowed to shoot bullfrogs on a Sunday.
- In Arizona the bullfrog-hunting season is permanently closed.
- In Vermont you can be fined if your pig runs in a public park without the permission of a selectman.
- French Lick Springs, Indiana, once passed a law requiring all black cats to wear bells on Friday the 13th.
- In Foxpoint, Wisconsin, it is illegal for dogs to bark profusely, snarl, or make any menacing gestures.
- In Texas it's illegal to put graffiti on someone else's cow.
- In Lang, Kansas, it is illegal to ride a mule along Main Street in August, unless it is wearing a straw hat.
- In Berea, Kentucky, horses are not allowed on the streets and highways at night unless the animal has a bright red taillight securely attached to its "tail."
- In Tahoe City, California, horses may not wear cowbells.
- In Burns, Oregon, horses are allowed into taverns, if they pay an admission fee.
- In Wanassa, New Jersey, a dog is breaking the law if it is heard to be "crying."

If you enjoyed

Take Two Aspirin. . .and Call Me in Hawaii
be sure to check out

In the Marry Month:

The Best Wedding and Marriage Jokes and Cartoons

from The Joyful Noiseletter

Marriage offers endless opportunities for laughter—and this collection of wedding and marital humor, drawn from the files of *The Joyful Noiseletter*, is sure to please. Scores of jokes and humorous stories, all relating to the beloved institution of marriage, are categorized into chapters and accompanied by the cartoons of talented Christian artists. In the *Marry Month* is the first title in a planned quarterly release of joke books—arriving in plenty of time for the summer wedding season. This hilarious collection of marital mirth is ideal for couples, pastors, anyone looking for clean, good-humored content they can trust.

ISBN 978-1-61626-277-8 • Mass market paperback
192 pages • $4.99